The 7 Triggers to YES

"A fascinating window into how we really influence others' decisions and behaviors. Armed with this new scientific knowledge anyone can become a more effective leader and manager by efficiently producing results through others."

—Donald F. Donahue,
president, National Securities Clearing Corporation;
chief operating officer, The Depository Trust & Clearing Corporation;
and president, The Depository Trust Corporation

"As one of many professionals whose work depends on the basic psychological principles outlined by Freud, I see daily proof that personal reactions, decisions, and perceptions are driven by emotions, which become rationalized after the fact. Brain imaging now offers concrete evidence. Using the latest technological data, Granger gives the complex art of persuasion the ease of paint-by-numbers clarity and a process for success."

—Leslie Schweitzer Miller, M.D.,
New York University Psychoanalytic Institute

"By applying the principles and system Granger provides, businesses and organizations can run more effectively and more efficiently. With willing compliance, the seven triggers will help people get things done more quickly, more easily, and with better results."

—Michael J. Iandolo, president and general manager,
Lucent Technologies Mobility Solutions

"Recent advances in brain imaging research provide a much clearer picture of what actually motivates an individual's actions. Granger has transformed this research into a readily understandable and workable program that enables the reader to apply that information to his or her chosen career and produce desired results when interacting with others. Regardless of your organizational role or position, when you need to persuade, *The 7 Triggers to YES* shows you how in a new and highly effective way."

—Robert H. Miller, former president and CEO,
Charles of the Ritz Group, Ltd.

"The lessons learned here should be a great help to any budding diplomat or politician."

—Nicholas Rey, United States Ambassador to Poland, 1993–1997

"Bravo! I couldn't put it down. As a technically trained MBA, I made business presentations for years using logic, reason, and a wealth of data. I now see there is a more effective and much more efficient way to persuade and influence others. I'm giving a copy to my architect son, who like all of us, needs to persuade successfully."

—Josiah Stevenson, former director of development,
Dartmouth College

"Russ has assembled an impressive army of thought leaders on the subject of persuasion. Instead of telling the reader, he's softly selling the reader on the world's collective wisdom on what it really takes to persuade and win. A great read."

—Gerhard Gschwandtner, founder and publisher, *Selling Power*

"We had a saying while I was Publisher of *TRAINING Magazine*: 'Sell the heart and the mind will follow!' It worked! But we really didn't know why. Granger has pulled the veils back to explain this persuasion skill in *The 7 Triggers to Yes*. He explains with complete clarity how the brain responds to decision-making stimuli, and how to appeal to basic needs and instincts. What a great formula! The book can be absorbed in a few hours, and with practice, will lead to years of success."

—Jerry C. Noack, retired publisher, *TRAINING Magazine*

"The book is pathbreaking. Implementation is the bane of management groups and teams. The book explains a framework to make implementation 100% effective in a short time frame and with total buy in. It's been a long time since a book on management has equaled the thrill while reading a good mystery. It was hard to put down."

—Shailesh Mor, director of ocean services,
Expeditors International, Delhi, India

"The book is so essential to our growth that I have passed it on to top management. *The 7 Triggers to YES* is essential to the success of both our own sales team and our independent agents. We see a lot of management and sales training—this is really cutting edge!"

—Sharon Denzler, CPCU, director of training,
All Risks Ltd. insurance company

"Getting a nod from your supervisor, your manager, or your board of directors, is all about getting 'Yes.' The book has introduced me to triggers which I can now proactively put into practice."

—Anand Chaturvedi, Bangalore, India

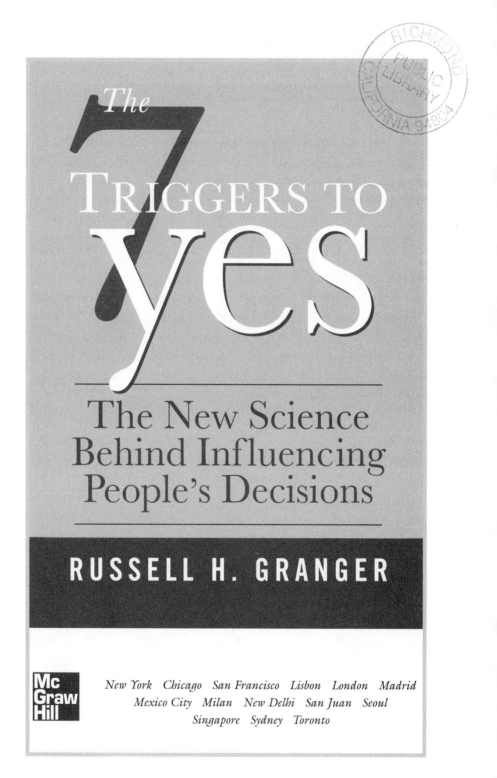

The
7
TRIGGERS TO
yes

The New Science
Behind Influencing
People's Decisions

RUSSELL H. GRANGER

Mc
Graw
Hill

New York   Chicago   San Francisco   Lisbon   London   Madrid
Mexico City   Milan   New Delhi   San Juan   Seoul
Singapore   Sydney   Toronto

The **McGraw·Hill** Companies

Copyright © 2008 by Russell H. Granger. All rights reserved. Printed in
the United States of America. Except as permitted under the United States
Copyright Act of 1976, no part of this publication may be reproduced or
distributed in any form or by any means, or stored in a database or retrieval
system, without the prior written permission of the publisher.

1 2 3 4 5 6 7 8 9 0 DOC/DOC 0 9 8 7

ISBN-13: 978-0-07-154437-5
MHID: 0-07-154437-2

McGraw-Hill books are available at special quantity discounts to use as
premiums and sales promotions, or for use in corporate training programs. For
more information, please write to the Director of Special Sales, Professional
Publishing, McGraw-Hill, Two Penn Plaza, New York, NY 10121-2298.
Or contact your local bookstore.

Library of Congress Cataloging-in-Publication Data

Granger, Russell H.
  The 7 triggers to yes / by Russell H. Granger.
    p. cm.
  Includes bibliographical references and index.
  ISBN 0-07-154437-2 (alk. paper)
  1. Business communication—Psychological aspects.   2. Persuasion
(Psychology)   3. Management—Psychological aspects.   I. Title.
II. Title: Seven triggers to yes.
HF5718.G73 2008
658.4'5—dc22   2007035871

This book is dedicated to Mom,
who provided the open atmosphere
for discussion and persuasion.

Contents

CONTENTS

CONTENTS

"We are not thinking machines—
we are feeling machines that think."

DR. RICHARD RESTAK,
neuropsychologist and author of
The Secret Life of the Brain

PREFACE

Inspiration to write this book occurred long before the scientific breakthroughs that enabled the process. From the time I was eight years old and winning prizes for persuading people to buy magazine and newspaper subscriptions, I have had an enthusiastic interest in persuasion. I took a college degree in psychology to learn more. After executive roles in large corporations, I formed a training company to share my knowledge and to help others become more successful.

The real impetus for the book began in the late 1980s based on a partnership with a then-vibrant AT&T. CEO Bob Allen recognized the need for better application of the elusive skill of persuasion. Allen provided millions to fund research in persuasion skills. This money was parceled out to top university graduate business schools who then conducted the research for AT&T. The research results were delivered to AT&T's training university. With the help and support of Jack Bowsher, recently retired director of corporate training at IBM, my company won the contract and the challenge to partner with AT&T to assimilate all this business school high-level research and create training programs from the research.

We learned some things that work in persuasion, but had no idea why or how they worked. The research provided experiential information, with much conjecture, speculation, and doctrine based on observation and extrapolation. The training programs were created, and worked reasonably well. But we were still not at the heart of how and why. The book was in the formulation stages, but totally lacking knowledge of how the brain really works in response to stimuli—to persuasion requests.

By the late 1990s the exciting advances in technology and scientific neurological discoveries began to shape and fine-tune the focus of the book. These discoveries produced many excellent books on brain processes and persuasion. But none offered a process, a system we could employ to apply this newly acquired knowledge. None really helped us become more successful at getting that all-important "Yes!" I have written this book to provide you with not only the breakthrough information, but to give you a complete system, a process that will enable you to achieve the results you seek with full compliance, agreement, and shared conclusions from others.

ACKNOWLEDGMENTS

The 7 Triggers to YES is the result of an incredible volume of research, hard work, and years of input by many people. The book exists in good part due to the intelligent help, support, organizational work, and diligence of my associate, Tristan DeSchepper. Tristan challenged everything, including my haste to get it done, with the admonition, "Let's do it right rather than fast." Thanks to Tristan we did it right rather than quickly. Well-meaning editors and authors suggested ways they would write this book—Tristan constantly reminded me, "This is your book—keep it yours." Thankfully, I followed his advice.

It's impossible to mention all who contributed to the development, the research, and the writing of the book. I'll offer my heartfelt thanks to just a few who made major contributions.

My daughter Jackie and her husband Mike provided lengthy real-world CEO review. They are responsible for enhancing and expanding the trigger units. Their suggestions provide easy to understand and easy to apply expanded content. Their input for the entire manuscript makes the book a much better read.

My son Russell's branding expertise, including work for major publishers, forced him to turn down every title I proposed for the book. He finally created the current title and brand. We now have a title and cover that best describes the book's content. The most important benefit from his input is that we have a stronger marketing message for the book, for future iterations of the book, and for the planned line extensions.

Bob Miller provided another CEO review, making suggestions to strengthen every chapter. His written notes and many meeting hours make the book more practical, more accurate, and more applicable for other leaders.

Dr. Richard Suprina provided an educator's touch and made many corrections and additions. His final note, "This is an A+," was a great motivator to ultimately warrant that evaluation.

Bob Dunnican, RWD Design, has been our go-to guy for forms and graphics for decades. His thoughtful approach for forms to make our systems work has been invaluable.

My wife, Janet, gave me the time and space to do my thing while she cared for all else. Herb Haschen freed me from many other obligations, allowing me to spend more time writing.

And finally, this book could not have been written without the help of the scientists who did the research leading to the incredible breakthroughs forming the heart and soul of this work. I am indebted to their long, hard, fascinating search to help determine how the brain truly works in real time, who we really are, and why we act as we do.

Chapter 1

The Awesome Power of Persuasion

W ho wields the world's greatest power? Who accomplishes their dreams?

The most successful people are those who can effectively get things done. They influence others to agree or comply, to effectively execute goals, objectives, and wishes. Success, perhaps survival, for you and for your organization hinges primarily on one skill: the power of persuasion—the ability to persuade people to say "yes," to willingly concur or follow your directions or act on your behalf. Power may be granted from bosses above you, yet execution and results are accomplished through your success in influencing others.

Persuaders rule. They always have and always will. Great persuaders have enormous power. They motivate change. Build successful teams. Revitalize entire organizations. They create growth and profit. They lead others to new heights. And they achieve personal goals for wealth, power, and influence. Every human interaction requires persuasion: the ability to influence cooperation, collaboration, and results. Great leaders motivate us. They ignite passion. They persuade us to act. The world's greatest achievements have been accomplished through persuasion.

OK. So persuasion is critical to success. We all know that. The question is, what do we know today about the process of persuasion that we didn't know before? What's different? What can we learn to become better persuaders? The difference is simple, dramatic, and, indeed, exciting. With the recent advent of live, real-time brain imaging technology, and with the resulting disciplines emerging in neuroscience, we have actually learned, for the first time, how the human brain processes information. Finally we know how we make, and how we influence, decisions that determine behaviors and actions. And what we've learned will forever change the way we interact with others.

In his book and five-part PBS TV series, *The Secret Life of the Brain,* Dr. Richard Restak, M.D., neurologist, neuropsychologist, researcher, and clinical professor of neurology at George Washington University Medical Center in Washington, D.C., offers us a real eye-opener. Restak, one of the world's top neurological scientists, recipient of the Linacre Medal for Humanity and Medicine and of the Decade of the Brain Award, uses his chapter, "The Adult Brain," to distill our current brain research into the following blockbuster shown in the book's opening: "We are not thinking machines, we are feeling machines that think."

In another of his books, *Mozart's Brain and the Fighter Pilot,* Restak puts the new knowledge in overall context, summing up the best information we have to date about brain function and how we actually process sensory input to the brain:

> Despite popular notions to the contrary, the brain does not operate like a computer or any other machine. That's why we have to stop forcing it to act in ways that are unnatural and unproductive. Your brain is not a logic machine. As it turns out, emotions and feelings about something or someone occur *before* you've made any attempt at conscious evaluation.

This is strong stuff! For several thousand years we've primarily been taught, at least in educated society, to use logic and reason to influence decisions and actions. Yet all this time even the most sophisticated among us have typically been forcing the brain to act in unnatural, unproductive ways. Not smart! The good news is there's a better way to persuade, to influence, to gain compliance, to obtain commitment on decisions and actions that are in the best interests for all concerned.

HIT OR MISS, TRIAL AND ERROR

Sure, salespeople, advertisers, and others have been using emotional appeals for years. But it's been hit and miss. We've been working on instinct or hard-fought trial-and-error efforts. Now we have solid facts to help us become consciously competent in the science of persuasion. The better we understand how our brains process information, the better we'll be able to communicate with others—doing so not in a manner that works *against* the brain but in a way that employs our natural brain process.

As science evolves we're coming to realize that our standard approaches to persuasion have been completely wrong. Most of us have learned to persuade by using the best arguments, the best data, and the best information available; all presented in a logical and rational manner to generate the thinking, decisions, and actions we seek. Business leaders—actually most of us—believe that our peers rely heavily on logic and reason to make their decisions and inform their actions. Suddenly, to everyone's amazement, we're learning that the brain just doesn't work this way.

In *Business to Business* magazine, Emory University business school professor Joseph Reiman writes:

> Neuroimaging technology allows us to measure brain activity and it does so more accurately because neurons don't lie. These little guys, neurons, all ten billion of them, prove there is a chemical and biological basis for

how we behave, and their message is: *business behaves wrongly.*

Wow! That's quite a statement—that we now know the chemical and biological basis for how we behave.

And with that knowledge, we know what we've been doing wrong—and more important, we know what we can do better to influence others. So if we are not thinking machines, if we are not primarily influenced by logic and cognitive reasoning, how do we make decisions? And more important, how do we influence the decisions of others? The answers are fully developed in this book. However, put simply, we each have internal databases that provide us with the ability to immediately feel the right response to outside stimuli.

From birth, we build our own internal databases that form our personal self-guidance system. This system automatically triggers our best responses to external stimuli. Our triggers are embedded in our brains; they belong specifically to each of us. Triggering "yes" is a process in which we help others—our persuasion partners— activate their own decision-making navigation systems.

WHO NEEDS PERSUASION SKILLS?

Dr. Condoleezza Rice graduated college cum laude and Phi Beta Kappa at age 19 from the University of Denver. Her experience in positions of power led her to claim: "Power is nothing unless you can turn it into influence." Her thoughts are echoed by Harvard Business School Professor Michael D. Watkins: "Formal authority and other resources of leadership are never sufficient to get things done. Leaders need the power to persuade."

Leaders, executives, managers, line and staff personnel each succeed or fail in proportion to the individual's skill of persuasion.

Each must influence and gain compliance from those up, down, and across every strata of the organization. And yes, let's include suppliers and clients among those we need to persuade.

We often think we can get results by *telling* people what to do. Can't CEOs, executives, and managers do that? Don't we tell our kids, our spouses what we want done? Can't the president of the United States just tell people what to do and get it done? Not according to President Harry S. Truman who said, "I sit here all day trying to persuade people—that's all the powers of the president amount to."

Richard Neustadt, in his book *Presidential Power and the Modern Presidents,* writes, "In these words of a president, spoken on the job, one finds the problem now before us: 'powers' are no guaranty of power."

Neustadt adds, "There is a widely held belief in the United States that a reasonable president would need no power other than the logic of his argument." But logic just doesn't cut it—even for the president. And when Neustadt wrote: "Presidential power is the power to persuade," he forced us to reconceptualize the presidency.

HARD SCIENCE

Dr. Robert Cialdini, a well-known psychologist studying persuasion, writes in *Harvard Business Review:* "No leader can succeed without mastering the art of persuasion. But there's a hard science in that skill, and a large body of psychological research suggests that there are basic laws of winning friends and influencing people."

That "hard science" and "psychological research" form the breakthrough knowledge for this book. We have documented scientific knowledge about the way to persuade, to influence, to get the results we seek. Neuroscience recently discovered stunning information about how the human brain functions for decision making, persuasion, behaviors, and actions. We really do understand, finally, why we act as we do in response to stimuli.

By opening these pages, you've taken the first step to persuasion success. Now you can use your own genius to learn and apply the shared information. You can become an excellent persuader, a leader who makes great things happen. You can be one of an elite group staying well ahead of the success curve. This new science and psychological research will change forever the ways we interact with other people, how we manage them, and how we influence their decisions, behaviors, and actions.

The business community has long been well aware that persuasion is a skill critical to personal and business success. "The seemingly magical power to persuade has always been important," we read in a piece by George W. Pratt in the *Harvard Business Review*, "but it's critical now with flatter management structures, cross functional teams and intercompany partnerships. Everyone, whether a leader or individual contributor must be able to influence."

BETTER WAYS TO SUCCEED THROUGH PERSUASION

How will you personally benefit from acquiring brand-new, scientifically based persuasion skills? You'll be better equipped to accomplish your goals. These accomplishments will likely come more easily and quickly as you use more effective ways to obtain full agreement, commitment, and willing execution from others. You will favorably influence the actions of those up, down, and across every level of your organization. And, of course, great persuasion skills will positively impact every level of your social and personal life as well. You will be better positioned to achieve the things you want with and through others.

ORGANIZATIONAL GAINS

How will your organization benefit from applying this new science toward persuasion? Professor Jay Conger, former director of the Leadership Institute at the University of Southern California, lends context: "Like power, persuasion can be a force for enormous good in an organization. It can pull people together, move ideas forward, galvanize change and forge constructive relationships."

As Conger astutely adds, "The necessary art of persuasion, the language of leadership, is misunderstood, underutilized, and more essential than ever."

Asserting that the language of leadership—persuasion—is "misunderstood" and "underutilized" says a great deal about our current limited state of persuasion knowledge. Yet it's not our fault. Until now we just didn't have the scientific knowledge of brain function.

Better persuasion skills—convincing people to do what must be done—will help organizations save time and energy through greater efficiency. With fewer ruffled feathers, companies, organizations, and departments can operate more smoothly and get more done in less time.

The application of documented, scientifically based persuasion skills will enable better results by elevating every individual to a higher level of execution. The company will reach higher levels of morale, performance, cooperation, and goal achievement.

We know managers spend some 80 percent of their time communicating with others, trying to persuade them to do what needs to be done. Yet how well do they accomplish that persuasion requirement? Not very well, it turns out; mainly because we "misunderstood." We didn't know how our brains reacted to requests or to stimuli that required decisions. As indicated, one of the most interesting elements of the breakthrough information that follows is that it directly contradicts what most of us believe about the persuasion and decision-making process. While we are called upon daily to make things happen through others, most of us still don't have the foggiest idea how to effectively persuade people.

"Persuasion," Professor Watkins says, "is a core leadership skill." The author of *The Leadership Triad*, Dale Zand, puts a sharper edge on the leadership requirement, noting, "You can't be a leader if you can't influence others to act." And, as Cialdini adds, "Persuasion skills exert a far greater influence over others' behavior than formal power structures do."

OK. So persuasion is a critical, requisite core leadership skill and we understand that the current persuasion methods are antiquated, misunderstood, and inadequate. Can we teach people the new, more informed approach, and, if so, will those involved learn how to persuade more effectively, more efficiently? The scientific and academic communities have answered with a resounding "Yes!"

"Good news from behavioral science," *Harvard Business Review* writes. "Persuasion works by appealing to deeply rooted human needs. We can learn to secure consensus, cut deals, win concessions by artfully employing scientific principles of influencing people. By understanding how to predictably meet deep seated human needs, anyone can strengthen [his or her] persuasive powers."

And here's even better news from Cialdini's article in *HBR*: "Persuasion is grounded in basic scientific, practical and learnable principles."

The "deeply rooted human needs," the "practical and learnable principles" are now understood by the new science of "real-time" brain function—in vivo neurophysiology. We know scientifically how the human brain processes decision-making information. And by learning and applying this knowledge we can enhance our results, our lives, our very being.

EQ AND IQ

The new knowledge for successfully dealing with people is gaining traction in the business community and has spawned a bevy of books and courses about an all-inclusive term with growing business awareness—Emotional Quotient, or EQ, also referred to as Emotional Intelligence. This differentiates high IQ from high EQ. And guess what—studies show that leaders, executives, and managers with high EQ produce better business results than those with high IQ.

A recent survey of business leaders conducted by the American Management Association asked what skills were most needed to effectively lead others. The top two skills were: (1) communication skills and (2) the ability to motivate and inspire others.

Isn't that how we get things done? Isn't it how we persuade? Interestingly, documentation reveals that even among those with high IQ, the absence of EQ contributes to poor performance. One international study by the worldwide executive search firm Egon Zehnder International found that although most people are hired because of high IQ, most are terminated because of low EQ.

EQ is a broad term, yet the critical element of EQ is understanding how other people process and react to emotional input. With that knowledge we can focus our leadership in the right direction and enhance our own EQ. Why is this knowledge so critical to our personal and business success? The answer is readily apparent— we can effectively influence others' decisions only when we understand how others process information to make decisions.

THE THREE OPTIONS TO "YES"

Let's take a step back. How can we get things done with and through others? What means do we each have to produce the actions and results we seek? Our choices are fairly limited. We have basically three options:

- Use force.
- Negotiate for the results we seek.
- Persuade to gain compliance and action.

In today's business world, force is outmoded and ineffectual. We can demand that people do our bidding, and perhaps even force them to act. This may produce action, but certainly not willing compliance. And without positive, willing compliance we likely won't get the results we expect.

Negotiation is a give-and-take, time-consuming process. It takes a great deal of skill and requires each party to bargain, to give something up to get something in return. It's a process where two people often get what neither wants. Negotiation authors and gurus tell us to negotiate *only* when all other means for accomplishment are exhausted. By contrast, persuasion is the only way to get full agreement, compliance, willing attitudes, decisions, behaviors, actions, and desired results.

SHARED SOLUTIONS

What, then, is the magic of "persuasion"? How can we best define this term we often use almost interchangeably with such words as "influence" and "convincing"? At USC, Dr. Conger provides perhaps the simplest, most straightforward definition in his article from the *Harvard Business Review* called "The Necessary Art of Persuasion": "Effective persuasion becomes a process by which the persuader leads colleagues to a problem's shared solution."

The key words are "shared solution," and "process." "Shared solution" refers to results in everyone's best interest. "Process" indicates that persuasion is not an off-the-cuff bag of psychological tricks you can immediately apply to any situation. Thus persuasion is not an event; instead, it's a full-fledged process that will unfold as we go forward. Persuasion is understanding human nature and the human brain, then working in concert with natural processes.

Historically, the term "rhetoric" has been used to define methods for gaining commitment and desired action. Aristotle (384–322 BCE) in his *Rhetoric, Book One* (of three) defines rhetoric as "discovering the best available means of persuasion." Science has finally provided us with the breakthrough, a documented approach to providing "the best available means of persuasion."

PERSUASION—MYTH AND REALITY

Some uninformed people might view persuasion in a pejorative context. Some see persuasion as an element in the "hard sell" category. Others equate persuasion with manipulation and deception. "Persuasion supersedes sales and is quite the opposite of deception," Conger writes. Like money, power, or position, persuasion can be employed for good or evil. Yet when we strive for a "shared solution," persuasion is the opposite of manipulation. As we learn more about the ways the brain processes information, we will see that the new art and science of persuasion works with the brain's internal guidance systems rather than against them. Working in concert with the other person's natural brain processes is the opposite of manipulation.

Persuasion is motivating someone to do something they might not do if you didn't ask. Persuasion aims to win both the heart and the mind, and must therefore induce attitude, emotion-based change. It's the skill of changing attitudes, motivating behaviors, and generating decisions for a shared solution. When one has influenced another's attitudes, feelings, decisions, behaviors, and actions, persuasion has occurred.

Harvard Business Review provides its own definition: "Persuasion doesn't mean begging, cajoling or manipulating. Quite the contrary, it's how we get things done through others—no matter who we are."

Persuasion has nothing to do with arm-twisting, nor does it depend on charisma or personality. Rather, persuasion is the application of the right information, the stimuli that will be accepted and acted upon by the other person's own internal self-guidance systems.

Persuasion is partnering with people to achieve mutual goals and benefits. Persuasion is a process that will turn your own thoughts, goals, and dreams into tangible reality. And the good news: persuasion is a skill anyone can master quickly.

What's the difference between the way we try to persuade today and the new science that will forever change our approach to influencing others and gaining their compliance? Has anything really changed?

Ever had a great idea? One that might produce excellent results for you and your organization? Ever had a need to get things done through others? Ever wanted something that someone could do for you? Have you always been successful in getting the best results from these ideas and needs? If not, I'm going to help you accomplish such ends. This book—combining a distillation of 2,500 years of persuasion research (since our earliest studies of rhetoric) along with today's remarkable scientific findings about the human brain's decision-making process—will make you a successful persuader, one who can get others to willingly execute your wants and needs.

A TESTED, DOCUMENTED PROCESS

Here's where this book differs from the spate of other excellent books on the science of persuasion and the brain. I will share the information with you relating to the new science; but, more important, I provide you with a fully tested, proven process to implement this knowledge. This is a complete "How To" book to make you consciously competent as a formidable persuader. You will be a better leader because you'll know how to get others to follow. You'll get things done with and through others. You will have a full understanding of how decisions are made, and you will learn how to trigger the other person's internal guidance system to produce shared results.

I'll then show you:

- How to effectively organize and frame your presentation.
- How to deliver a successful persuasive presentation.
- How to turn resistance into opportunity.
- How to facilitate the ultimate decision to comply, to say "yes," to act.

This is the first book to provide the knowledge, the skills, and the process for the "hard science" approach to achieving successful leadership persuasion results. As noted, this approach begins with a new understanding:

- The brain is not a computer; it doesn't operate as one.
- Your brain is not a logic machine.
- We have to stop forcing the brain to act in ways that are unnatural and unproductive.
- Emotions and feelings occur before you've made any attempt at conscious evaluation.

PARTNERS IN PERSUASION

Persuasion is a shared process and the goals should become the same for you and the other person. In reality, you and the person you are persuading become partners in generating shared decisions and actions to reach a meaningful goal. Thus we refer to the person you are persuading as your "partner." You are partners in pursuing the same goal—the shared resolution of an idea.

I'll do my best to be your partner in acquiring better persuasion skills. My personal background includes a degree in psychology, a track record of successful management consulting and training, and a lifelong study into how we get results with and through others.

Several of the examples we share in the book come from my personal experience as an executive of a multi-billion-dollar financial services corporation, as president of my own training company, and from my experience as a management consultant to Fortune 500 corporations. The examples are real. They happened. I hope you can interpolate from these examples ways in which you can produce the same results.

Why will this book be invaluable to you? As noted well by Dr. Jay Conger, we have a clear, succinct answer: "The necessary art of persuasion, the language of leadership, is misunderstood and underutilized. If there ever was a time for business people to learn the fine art of persuasion, it is now."

I'll take you on the persuasion quest from ancient Greece on to the Roman Empire, through thousands of years of psychology and persuasion guesswork, then into today's breakthrough neurological scientific discoveries. From there we'll share an easy-to-learn process for successful persuasion execution. Let's begin the journey!

REVIEW AND REFERENCE

- Success for you and your organization hinges primarily on the skill of persuasion—the ability to get others to say yes, to willingly follow your directions and act on your behalf.
- Power may be granted from bosses above you, but execution and results are accomplished by persuading others. Power is nothing without persuasion.

- Leaders, even the president of the United States, cannot succeed without the core leadership skill of persuasion.
- We can effectively influence others' decisions only when we understand how others process decision-making information.
- Emotional Quotient (EQ) is understanding how people process and react to emotional input. Those with high EQ produce better results than those with high IQ.
- We've been primarily taught to persuade using data, logic, and rational arguments. This approach doesn't work well because the brain doesn't make decisions this way.
- Persuasion is not an event, it's a process. Persuasion is understanding human nature and the human brain, then working with the brain's natural processes.
- We have three options to get things done with and through others: force, negotiation, and persuasion.
  - Force may produce action but not willing compliance.
  - Negotiation is a process where two people often get what neither wants.
  - Persuasion is the best way to get full agreement, compliance, decisions, actions, and results.
- The new art and science of persuasion works with the brain's internal guidance systems rather than against them. We strive for a shared solution—the opposite of manipulation or deception. Persuasion is partnering with people to achieve mutual goals and benefits.
- For your CPO, current persuasion opportunity, we have an interactive form to help determine the most persuasive elements that you could tap into. Go to www.seventriggers.com where you can select the applicable elements, make notes, print them out.

Chapter 2

Winners and Losers

The greatest historical achievements are the results of persuasion. The empire builders, the Caesars and Napoleons, won by persuading others to follow. Cities and civilizations were built with persuasion. Columbus persuaded Queen Isabella that he could reach the East, India, by sailing west; then persuaded her to finance his ships. Once a slave, Frederick Douglass wrote, "If I can persuade, I can move the universe." He persuaded Lincoln to issue the Emancipation Proclamation. JFK persuaded Congress and the American public to support and fund a plan to put an American on the moon.

But what happens when people can't persuade? Right—nothing!

Lack of persuasive power is a key factor in keeping otherwise outstanding people from achieving the success they deserve. Many great inventions—historical solutions, major medical advances, critical corporate change initiatives—fail simply because the creator hadn't acquired easy-to-learn persuasion skills. Are you smart—maybe flat-out brilliant? Do you have degrees from a top university? Do you have ideas that might change your life . . . significantly improve your organization's status . . . change the world for the better? You're sure to be a success—right? Well, maybe not. Gifted intelligence, great ideas, and outstanding products by themselves do not persuade. Even the most amazing scientific discoveries didn't see the light of day until someone *persuaded* someone else to get a discovery into the marketplace.

A TIGER BY THE TAIL

Chester F. Carlson was a brilliant physicist, lawyer, patent attorney, inventor, and research engineer. He was also a pitiful persuader. His first persuasion job was to sell himself as a newly minted physicist from the prestigious California Institute of Technology, and he failed miserably. He contacted 82 companies, got interviews, but was unable to persuade even one of those companies to hire him. Carlson kept studying, earned more degrees, and finally got work with Bell Labs in New York. But he was going nowhere.

Working in Bell Labs' patent department, Carlson had to manually retype patent descriptions and recreate patent drawings for required copies. He sought a better way to save on the time and boredom. He tinkered on the side, hoping to make his big break. Then, in 1937, in his Jackson Heights, New York–kitchen, using the principles of photoconductivity, Carlson invented and patented the world's first photocopy process.

Even so, years passed without Carlson getting anyone interested in his invention.

In 1939 he said, "I knew I had a very big tiger by the tail." But because he wasn't skilled in persuasion, that tiger remained fast asleep. Comatose! Despite inventing a process that would spawn an industry and forever transform the way the world does business, Carlson couldn't get anyone to back the project—he couldn't even get anyone to take it on as a product. Year after year he tried desperately to persuade companies that he had something of value. He met with IBM, Kodak, GE, and RCA. Twenty companies in all—not a nibble. Then, in 1959, a company known as Haloid introduced the first commercial unit based on Carlson's design, Copier Model 914.

Two years later, Haloid became the Xerox Corporation and the copier industry was born.

Carlson had created an incredible product—but lacking persuasive skills it took him 22 years to get anyone interested! Twenty-two years from patented product to production. Amazing! A brilliant, highly needed, world-changing product—the forerunner of computer printers and fax machines—went absolutely nowhere for more than two decades. Is persuasion important? You bet it is! History is rife with examples of persuaders winning and nonpersuaders losing. The secret of success is not merely to have great ideas, products, or solutions; the secret is to learn to *persuade* others to comply and execute.

THE TWO-TRILLION-DOLLAR INVENTION

Jack St. Clair Kilby invented something far more important than Carlson's copier. While at Texas Instruments Kilby received patent number 3643138 for his invention of the first integrated circuit, the forerunner of today's computer chip. Impressive, right? No! Kilby couldn't even persuade his own company to implement the idea. "Don't you realize," he was asked by management, "that computers are getting bigger, not smaller?"

Because he, too, was a nonpersuader, for years his brilliant invention went undeveloped. In his untitled autobiography written for the 2000 Nobel Committee, Kilby admits, "I worked hard with Robert Royce at Fairchild Semiconductor to achieve commercial acceptance." But that didn't happen. Even his savvy engineering skills could not persuade anyone to put his invention into any commercial application. Instead, Kilby acknowledged wistfully: "The integrated circuit provided much of the 'entertainment' at major technical meetings over the next few years." The most important element in today's entire electronic field provided merely "technical entertainment" as banter and ridicule. For four years his invention went absolutely nowhere, and thence was used only as a small component in the Minuteman Missile.

For six more years Kilby couldn't persuade anyone he had something of value. In truth, he never did convince anyone of this value. Then, a decade after obtaining his patent, Kilby was asked to make a calculator small enough to fit into a pocket. Using his integrated circuit, he invented the digital calculator and the chip had its first commercial application. Others saw the potential applications and a new electronics era was born. But Kilby's lack of persuasive ability had kept this major technological breakthrough in the dark for more than a decade!

Today the chip Kilby invented forms the heart of every computer in the world, every cell phone, every video game, every digital camera, every MP3 player, and a host of other forms of electronic wizardry. In 2000, 42 years after patent issue for his invention, Kilby received, among many other awards, the Nobel Prize for physics. Yet for a decade his invention lay fallow. Today the value of the goods powered by his chip is almost $2 trillion.

Two critical inventions—the copy machine and the integrated circuit chip—went nowhere for many years because their genius creators weren't persuaders.

PERSUASION NATURALS

But flip a coin. Try the other side. Let's look at a situation where a great persuader had no product, only limited experience, and no credibility—not even a college degree. Yet, with persuasion, he would become the world's richest man.

In 1975 Bill Gates was studying pre-law at Harvard. Meanwhile, his hobby was playing with early computers. Gates and boyhood friend Paul Allen noticed that the Micro Instrumentation and

Telemetry Systems Company (MITS) had developed one of the first mini computers—the Altair 8080. Gates contacted MITS and told them he had developed a BASIC program that would make their computer run better. It was a lie. He had nothing. Yet he persuaded the company to install his program in their computer. Gates had never seen the Altair 8080 and had never written a line of BASIC code. He didn't even have the computer's operating chip. Yet—with his persuasive ability—he convinced MITS to purchase a product that didn't exist. Working around school assignments, for eight weeks Gates wrote code. He then flew to the MITS office and installed the untested program in a computer he had not seen until that day. To even his surprise, it worked perfectly! MITS now owned the newest BASIC program.

What next for Gates? Well, he simply persuaded MITS to sell him its BASIC program! Still a Harvard pre-law student, he realized the software industry was in its birthing stage. He next persuaded his parents to let him drop out of Harvard, and persuaded Paul Allen to join him in a two-man venture. Microsoft was born. And Gates has since been described as the most influential person of the twentieth century and beyond. Persuasion is influence!

By contrast, Carlson had everything but persuasive ability. He had an incredible product, patented and ready to go. He had impeccable credentials. Yet he was flat-out stymied for 22 years. Gates—with little but an idea, a keen technical mind, and inherent persuasion skills—quickly built the Microsoft empire. He started a company on an idea and persuasion.

Can persuasion save a moribund company? Lido Anthony Iacocca is a legend in persuasion. With a persuader's understanding of consumer thinking, he convinced Ford to build an entirely new concept car—the Mustang. It broke all car sales records. He did the same with the minivan at Chrysler, initiating the van and SUV industry.

Yet the ultimate triumph of Lee Iacocca's persuasive prowess was with the United States Congress. In 1979 the immense Chrysler Corporation, drowning in debt, was on its deathbed. The banks were calling their loans, would not extend them further, and the company faced almost certain bankruptcy. Chrysler had one "long shot" last hope—a government bailout loan guaranty which virtually everyone opposed. In August of that year, many of the country's leading newspapers editorialized negatively about the proposed bailout. On August 2, Thomas A. Murphy, chairman of General Motors, publicly opposed any financial assistance from the government. On August 10, Secretary of the Treasury G. William Miller made public *his* opposition to financial support for Chrysler.

Then, against staggering odds, Iacocca personally made an incredibly persuasive presentation to both houses of the U.S. Congress. He used every persuasion trigger in his arsenal. He was simply magnificent. On December 18, the House of Representatives approved the Chrysler Corporation Loan Guaranty Act of 1979. Iacocca persuaded 241 representatives to vote "yes," overriding only 124 "nays." One day later the U.S. Senate voted 43 to 34 to approve the act. On December 23, the Senate and House conferees approved and cleared the $3.5 billion Chrysler aid package for the president's approval.

Iacocca's persuasive ability single-handedly saved the Chrysler Corporation from extinction.

Iacocca often acknowledged that there were thousands of people who knew more about cars than he did. But then he'd add, "I know more about people." Innately he knew how to persuade.

Chrysler took only $1.2 billion of the $3.5 billion government guaranty Iacocca had structured, and paid back the entire amount in less than four years. Iacocca's persuasion produced positive results for all concerned. At the same time, he set new, far-reaching precedents for congressional interaction with industry.

Persuasion can also grow a company. Jack Welch, former CEO of General Electric, was named the most successful business leader of the twentieth century. Welch is the consummate persuader. He took a stodgy, stagnant company and forged it into a financial juggernaut—today's General Electric. In his autobiography *Jack: Straight from the Gut,* Welch shares a remarkable revelation: "Nearly everything I've done in my life has been accomplished with other people." Welch knows he didn't personally accomplish GE's incredible ascendancy to growth and profit. Wisely, he persuaded others to make it happen. And they did! To accomplish his extraordinary leadership feats, he capitalized on a few very basic persuasion principles: a few triggers that worked incredibly well. You'll soon learn how Welch created conformity, commitment, and spectacular results.

Perhaps the quintessential persuader of our time is The Donald. While a student at Wharton Business School, Trump and his father purchased a bankrupt apartment complex. To purchase and renovate the property, Trump persuaded lenders to finance the project at considerably more than the purchase price. Without a penny of his own invested, The Donald and his father purchased, renovated, then made the complex highly successful. Donald Trump learned early on that all you need to get ahead is the skill of persuasion.

Trump then moved to Manhattan to make his mark on the world. To make the requisite contacts he needed access to the movers and shakers. Trump felt the way to accomplish this was to join an exclusive club. He was told Le Club was the place to rub elbows with the captains of industry, the rich and famous. But membership in Le Club was not open to the public and was very difficult to obtain. Not knowing a single member who might sponsor him, Trump sought out, then wined and dined the club manager, finally persuading him to provide membership.

Trump had a weak resumé, little experience, and few personal financial resources. But now he had contacts. With the sheer force of persuasion he created some of the biggest deals New York City has ever seen. He arranged options on the rail yards of the long-gone Penn Central Railroad. Then, at age 28, he persuaded the city to use his optioned land to build the city's Convention Center. He came very close to having it named The Trump Convention Center! The memory of the late Senator Jake Javits won that one.

Next Trump optioned the property of the Commodore Hotel and persuaded the city to give him something it had never before given—the granting of a 40-year tax abatement. He then convinced the Hyatt Corporation to join him in building a prime hotel on the site. He then persuaded Manufacturers Hanover Bank to finance a $70 million construction loan. The magnificent Grand Hyatt Hotel became a New York landmark and Trump became a multimillionaire. Friend and foe alike agree that no one will ever again persuade New York City to grant a 40-year tax abatement. And of course the whole world has learned more about The Donald since he persuaded a very skeptical NBC to pilot a crazy new idea for a show to be called *The Apprentice*.

But here's the strange thing. If people used logic and due diligence, they would avoid Trump like the plague. Investors in his casinos and hotel companies have fared poorly; he has been involved in many business and personal bankruptcies; his hotel casino business is constantly in and out of bankruptcy. Shares that sold for more than $35 were later worth just north of 35 cents. Yet The Donald is still a billionaire. He travels in his jets, his helicopters, and his limousines. He is The Donald.

Why does Trump continue to succeed? In a cover article, *Selling Power* magazine called Trump's ongoing success a marvel because, "It is constructed on a base of fantasy that his growing base of fans continue to buy into, blithely ignoring all evidence to the contrary." Evidence, logic, and rational thought take a back seat to the enormous power of emotional persuasion. Trump has an uncanny ability to capitalize on his ethos and pathos to negate any amount of logic. Like Bill Gates, he didn't have or need a product or service to climb the heights. Persuasion did it all.

PERSUADE OR PERISH

For 2,500 years the art and science of persuasion have attracted the world's best minds. Leaders ask: How do I motivate others to act? How do I generate change? How do I make things happen with and through others? These questions have challenged the thinkers and doers since antiquity. History's winners knew intuitively how to persuade and motivate others. They didn't know it at the time, but they applied scientific principles we now understand. We're going to share the information to allow you to consistently, effectively gain commitment, decisions, and desired results.

It matters little how necessary, creative, innovative, outstanding, or even critical your ideas, solutions, visions, or products are. If you can't convince someone to execute, you won't succeed. Persuade, motivate, gain compliance, and your ideas might well catapult you into fame, fortune, and self-fulfillment.

REVIEW AND REFERENCE

- The greatest historical achievements, including many empires and civilizations, are the results of persuasion. When people can't persuade, nothing happens.
- Lack of persuasive power keeps otherwise outstanding people from achieving success. Even the most amazing scientific discoveries didn't see the light of day until someone persuaded someone else to get the discovery into the marketplace.

- The secret of success is not merely to have great ideas, products, or solutions; the secret is to learn to persuade others to comply and execute.
- Chester Carlson invented and patented the first photocopy process. It took him 22 years to get his product from patent to production simply because he lacked persuasive ability.
- Jack Kilby invented the first integrated circuit, but couldn't even persuade his own company to back the idea. Trying for a decade, he couldn't get anyone to put his invention into practical use. Today his creation is the heart of a $2 trillion electronics industry.
- Two critical inventions, the copy machine and integrated circuit chip, went nowhere for many years because their genius creators weren't persuaders.
- Conversely, Bill Gates created the Microsoft empire on little but an idea and inherent persuasion skills.
- Lee Iacocca used his persuasive prowess to single-handedly save the Chrysler Corporation from extinction by persuading Congress to agree to an unheard-of government bailout loan guaranty.
- Jack Welch proved that persuasion can transform an entire company. He forged a stodgy, stagnant General Electric into today's financial juggernaut. Welch tapped into simple emotional triggers persuading staff to make it happen.
- Donald Trump with sheer force of persuasion built his own financial empire. If investors used logic and due diligence they would avoid Trump like the plague, yet The Donald is still a billionaire.
- Evidence, logic, and rational thought invariably take a back seat to the enormous power of emotional persuasion. It matters little how necessary, creative, or innovative your ideas, solu-

tions, or products are. If you can't persuade others to act, you won't succeed.

- For your CPO, current persuasion opportunity, we have an interactive form to help determine the most persuasive elements for your immediate persuasion goals. Go to www.seventriggers.com where you can select the applicable elements, make notes, print them out.

Chapter 3

Persuasion Then and Now

ow! After 2500 years, we get it! We finally know how the brain processes persuasion stimuli in real time.

To become a better leader, manager, or achiever, it's worth knowing a bit about persuasion, about where we've been and where we're going.

In discussing the importance of rhetoric, Aristotle got some things right. But not everything. Aristotle wrote that it is a "human failing" that we sometimes seem more persuaded by our emotions than by logic. The Greek philosopher believed, and taught, that we should be much more accepting of—and persuaded by—logic, reason, and rational cognitive thought. For Aristotle, logic and reason were the prime drivers for our decision making and our actions. For all those 2,500 years, most agreed with that thinking.

It was wrong!

Thus to understand the magnitude of today's breakthrough in persuasion and decision making, it's important to know the background of persuasion research. The background helps us understand how we got to where we are. More important, it helps us deal with some antiquated views that are still believed. A short history of persuasion sets the stage for today's breakthroughs. Knowing where we've been helps you better understand the breakthroughs in persuasion knowledge.

THE HISTORY OF PERSUASION

Persuasion is the world's oldest, most researched skill. Why? That's easy: *it's the world's most important skill!*

From the dawn of civilization we humans have pondered who we are and why we act as we do. We've long questioned the process behind our decisions, the ways decisions evolve, and how these decisions impact our thoughts and actions. We wonder how we ever made our own decisions and how we ever persuaded others to comply with them. We question the origins of our actions, and ask how we can more effectively influence the actions of others.

Scroll back in time to the fourth century BCE, when Athenians were experimenting with a new form of government. The Athenians quickly discovered that to succeed in a democracy they had to be persuasive. Leaders used persuasion, which they called rhetoric, to gain agreement or win support. Ordinary citizens used persuasion when pleading before a new legal body, the jury. Recognizing its profound importance, Athenian scholars, including Plato and Aristotle, began to study the powerful process of persuasion. At about this time, they defined three ways to persuade:

- *Logos,* the appeal to logic, reason, and facts.
- *Pathos,* the appeal to emotions.
- *Ethos,* the appeal of the speaker's authority, character, and credibility.

These scholars found that one or more of these appeals characterized any instance of persuasion.

From his research, Aristotle wrote three books about persuasion. Among his conclusions were that logic is the most reliable appeal, and persuasion should be based on logic and reason. He recognized that some are more persuaded by emotion, but, as noted, wrote that it is a "human failing" when we are persuaded more by emotion than by logic.

Ancient Greece proved persuasion so important—so effective in politics, commerce, jurisprudence, and everyday life—that when the Romans conquered Greece they continued to study and apply persuasion. Marcus Tullius Cicero became Rome's most prominent persuasion student. Cicero believed that a man would become great if he were the master of knowledge and persuasion. Cicero wrote that persuasion made knowledge useful.

Caesar Augustus became a master persuader. He magnificently used the ethos appeal, starting his speeches with "Vini, Vidi, Vici"—I came, I saw, I conquered. By establishing who he was and why people should listen to him, he won their support.

As the Greek and Roman empires declined, Christianity overpowered the old religions and governments. The reasoned, logical, skilled approach to persuasion was replaced by an omnipotent, omniscient dictum—the word of God, as interpreted by the church. No longer did the uneducated masses need to ponder persuasion or rational thought. The word of God was decreed to replace all reason, logic, and cognitive evaluation.

Logic, reason, and independent thought were harshly suppressed by the church. Scientists of the day were arrested, even murdered, in the name of Christianity. Copernicus (1473–1543) was arrested and branded a heretic for postulating that the earth revolved around the sun rather than the sun around the earth as the church preached. Copernicus' disciples, Galileo and Bruno, were severely punished by the church inquisitors. For his blasphemy about solar system revelations, and because of his refusal to recant, Christian inquisitors murdered Bruno, burned him at the stake in 1600. In 1633 the church, threatening Galileo with similar torture and death, forced him to renounce all his "heretical" views and sent him to prison for life. Persuasion, logic, and reason were strictly curtailed while the papacy firmly controlled knowledge and thinking.

In the Roman Church only St. Augustine recognized the need for one element of persuasion. In his *De Doctrina Christiana* he wrote that while Christians should not employ the sophist concept of persuasion, he understood that pathos, the appeal to emotions, was required to impart the church's "truths" and make them convincing. Interestingly, this awareness follows Aristotelian thinking that even facts and truth require persuasion to be believed and understood. Yet even St. Augustine was unable to extricate *persuasion* from the "off-limits box" Christianity had built around it.

In Renaissance Europe, for more than 200 years the study of persuasion, along with research into science and reason, was kept under tight wraps by the church. Finally, Friedrich Nietzsche (1844–1900), perhaps influenced by Martin Luther's attacks on the papacy, continued the revolution against the Roman church. Nietzsche's father was a pastor, yet Nietzsche developed a strong contempt for the control the Catholic Church had forced on humanity. He believed that the church had created and manipulated an environment where the highest intellectual values were labeled sinful and misleading. He began anew the study of persuasion and its connection to the emerging study of psychology, thus opening a new door to realistic scientific and philosophical thinking.

Meanwhile in the American colonies the study of rhetoric—persuasion—was taking root. As early as 1693, rhetoric was defined in a commencement speech at Harvard. In 1806 Nicholas Boylston bequeathed funds to establish a professorship of rhetoric at Harvard. John Quincy Adams was installed as chair. Aside from his academic approach to rhetoric, Adams was an accomplished natural persuader. At age 26 he talked his way into becoming the minister to the Netherlands—thence to Berlin, then Russia. As secretary of state under President Monroe, he persuaded Spain to cede Florida to the States. Adams finally persuaded the electorate to make him the sixth president of the United States.

Interestingly, the nineteenth century prescription for productive rhetoric was to follow Aristotle's advice on logic and reason. Logic was taught to be the best approach for creating rhetorical oratory, successful persuasion, and compliance. Finally, in the twentieth century we begin to see the merging of academia and practical approaches to persuasion. During this time we seem to have redis-covered the value and critical importance of getting others to comply with our wishes. Chaim Perelman (1912–1984) is one of the first to delve into the *New Rhetoric* of applying concepts and the-ories to the ever-present question—"How do we persuade others to do the things we want?" Perelman, recognized as a "rhetorical theorist," wrote many books on the subject of persuasion and was the earliest to break with thousands of years of tradition when he wrote, "One can be persuasive without being purely logical." A small step, but headed in the right direction! Perelman has been described as the person responsible for the marriage of rhetoric and pragmatics.

ECONOMY MOTIVATES PERSUASION RESEARCH

After World War II, the burgeoning economy prompted more research into ways for managers, leaders, and their followers to be more productive. To lead effectively, to compete successfully, man-agers had to persuade others to follow, to comply with their wishes. Carl I. Hovland of Yale University conducted groundbreaking research into ways to gain compliance and results through other people. Psychologists, academics, and business scholars had entered a race to determine how the process of persuasion works and how it can be applied more effectively. The search for real-world practicality for persuasion was in full swing.

During the last half of the twentieth century, psychologists conducted the first major, broad-based research into persuasion. Their emphasis was—as Aristotle said it should be—on the logical aspects. The research largely focused on cognition and rationality. From the 1950s through much of the 1990s, psychologists followed precedent and believed emotions were a disruptive force in the process of decision making and persuasion. Emotions were thought to inhibit rational thought. Most felt that emotions were primitive hangovers from the "flight or fight" days. In the decision and persuasion process, emotions were to be avoided. Higher forms of existence—rationality, foresight, logic, and cognitive thinking—were expected to win the day.

Throughout much of the twentieth century, high credence was given to the concept of will and to the power of will to control our thinking, our decision making, and our actions. The origins for these approaches to human action date back to St. Thomas Aquinas, through the "free will" of Immanuel Kant, and to twentieth-century researchers. The twentieth-century psychologists felt that internal feelings, wishes, and habits could, and should, be controlled by the will. They believed the will was an independent controller capable of directing emotion, thought, memory, learning, and decision making. The will could and should, it was suggested, suppress the subjective nature of emotion. None of the researchers through the twentieth century considered emotion as part of the rational, cognitive process. Ulric Neisser, in 1967, stated that emotion was one of the aspects of psychology not even considered in the rational, cognitive approach to our thought processes.

Many scientists determined that the processes of the brain and mind were far too complex to be explored intelligently. The psychologists in the behaviorist camp said the brain should be discounted because what goes on in the brain was not even worth consideration. What goes on inside the head couldn't be measured or evaluated, and we should rather explore our behaviors and actions, which can be documented and evaluated.

Thus, as noted, for 2,500 years the world's best, most brilliant minds could never have known that the human brain has some "ideas" of its own regarding the process of thinking, decision making, and persuasion. For all those years the secrets of brain function remained well guarded. The relationships between emotion and rational cognitive thinking, between decision making and actions, were hidden within the impenetrable amorphous mass of brain cells and synapses.

The Wizard was still behind the curtain.

REVIEW AND REFERENCE

- Aristotle believed that we should be more accepting of—and persuaded by—logic, reason, and rational thought. Until recently, most agreed that logic and reason are the prime drivers for our decisions and actions. They were wrong!
- In fourth century BCE Athenians learned that to succeed in a democracy they needed persuasion to gain agreement and support.
- Athenian scholars defined the three ways to persuade as:
  o *Logos*, the appeal to logic, reason, and facts.
  o *Pathos*, the appeal to emotions.
  o *Ethos*, the appeal of the speaker's character and credibility.
- Ancient Rome added to the Greek knowledge of persuasion. As the Roman Empire declined, Christianity overpowered research and free thought. Logic and reason were harshly suppressed by the church while the papacy firmly controlled "knowledge."
- Not until the early nineteenth century did the study of persuasion continue. During this time logic was still taught as the best approach to persuasion.

- After World War II, the burgeoning economy prompted more research into ways for managers, leaders, and their followers to be more productive. To lead effectively managers had to persuade others to follow, to comply with their wishes.
- During the last half of the twentieth century psychologists conducted the first major, broad-based research into persuasion. From the 1950s through the 1990s psychologists followed precedent and believed emotions were a disruptive force in the process of decision making and persuasion.
- Many scientists determined that the processes of the brain were far too complex to be explained intelligently. None of the researchers considered emotion a part of the rational, cognitive process. The relationship among emotion, rational thinking, and decision making remained hidden.
- For your CPO, current persuasion opportunity, we have an interactive form to help determine the most persuasive elements for your immediate persuasion goals. Go to www.seventriggers.com where you can select the applicable elements, make notes, and print them out.

Chapter 4

What's the Breakthrough?

For two and a half centuries of persuasion research the curtain remained closed to the realities of brain function. The curtain hid the true nature of the decision-making process and the application of that process to persuasion. During this period, persuasion research was stymied. The best we could accomplish was to create a set of unscientific, behaviorist concepts based on guessing.

The only tools available were observations of overt actions. We looked at consequences and attempted to define what preceded them, the antecedents. With this backward approach we generated inaccurate conclusions. With behaviorist observation to guide us we still based our persuasion attempts on spurious premises, the wrong antecedents. We hoped the brain would someday reveal those antecedents, yet the brain had remained mysterious—totally inaccessible. We could only learn from examining cadavers. We could dissect the physical brain and, doing so, learned brain anatomy, but little else.

The human brain has a volume of some 1,360 milliliters, and the neocortex has about 28 billion neurons, each connected to other neurons by tens of billions of synapse connections. Good information. Yet a dead, dissected brain tells us little about its real-time function. We learned the topography, but still had no road map.

We searched in vain for clues about brain functions. We wanted to know how we made decisions, how cognitive thinking, reason, and logic interacted with emotions. We wondered how these functions impacted our behavior. Most of all, we sought answers to the critical question: How do we impact others' brains, their decisions and actions? How do we persuade and influence others? How do we guide others' decision-making process? We knew the brain might some day yield its secrets, yet we had no way to access the answers we so desperately sought.

SCIENCE INTO THE ACT

During the late 1990s we saw a virtual explosion in brain research capabilities. Thanks to computer advances and new imaging technology, great opportunities arose. Until we knew how the brain really works, we could not know how our partner's brain worked and thus remained in the dark while seeking to persuade the best decisions. But if we learned how the brain functioned, we could apply that information to guide our partner's decision-making process to help him make the decisions we seek.

Science was stymied by the inability to observe brain function "in vivo," live, in real time. The new technologies have opened entirely new fields of science. By the 1990s scientists were unraveling the human genome. They were defining how our chromosomes and DNA affected our physical bodies. At the same time, neuroscientists began to explore real-time brain function to learn how this affected our thinking—yes, our virtual being! With the new technology, we dynamically lifted the curtain. We could now learn some of the brain's long-held, intensely guarded secrets.

The warp-speed quest forged ahead to determine not only how the brain functions but how decisions are made, how we influence ourselves, how we make judgments and decisions, and how we influence and persuade others.

NEW RESEARCH TOOLS

The combination of new technology, mega computers, and the newly formed scientific disciplines has enabled us finally to achieve the Holy Grail of neurological research. We found the new technologies allowing us to view in vivo brain processes so that we can indeed see the brain's processes work in real time.

These technologies include positron emission tomography (PET) scans, functional magnetic resonance imaging (fMRI), stereogeometric functional magnetic resonance spectroscopy (fMRS), and steady state probe topography (SSPT). Alone or in concert, they allow us to see, in real time, the pathways of brain processes. With these instruments in place we can provide a stimulus, then follow the thought paths, literally seeing the chemical flows to specific parts of the brain. For the first time we can apply stimuli and watch it activate decisions and actions.

We finally have the road map to go with the topography. For example, with SSPT, neurologists can tap into brain function with a noninvasive procedure that collects data from 64 sites on the scalp at a rate of 13 recordings per second from each site. That's 832 recordings per second! In a single minute we can now record 49,920 physical brain actions.

The value of the information gleaned from these technologies is gaining unprecedented acknowledgment and awareness. Books, magazine articles, and video series depicting this new awareness appear almost daily. While much of this information has been relegated to scientific journals, now even popular consumer publications are getting into the act. A recent issue of *National Geographic* contained a cover article on the new technology of brain research and function. The magazine cover shows a man with his scalp fully wired for in vivo exploration. *Time* magazine pictured the brain on its cover, followed by an article on brain function. And the information is trickling down. Graduate business schools and MBA curriculums for the first time offer courses on persuasion and brain function.

WATCHING THE BRAIN "LIGHT UP"

We have created a scientific, philosophical, and psychological breakthrough that will forever change the way we regard thought and decision processes. Using these tools, we can finally watch the brain as it processes stimuli. We can see specific parts of the brain "light up" as their functional elements are put into play. We can evaluate and scientifically measure physiological and psychological parameters of neural activation. We can objectively study brain functions that generate our moods, our thoughts, our decisions and actions. Learning how stimuli affect our everyday lives, we can now learn with reasonable certainty the best ways to lead others to employ their internal triggers to motivate the best decisions and actions.

These triggers will be fully defined as we progress, but for now we'll view triggers as elements in our own self-guidance systems. These elements trigger our decisions and actions in response to stimuli. The brain will either:

- Automatically activate an internal trigger for decision or action, or,
- If no trigger is activated, the brain will undertake cognitive evaluation.

As an example, when we see others clapping or cheering at an event, the brain triggers us to clap or cheer.

This scientific awareness of brain information flows provides a remarkable difference from the antiquated, unreliable behaviorist approach of watching human actions and attempting to extrapolate the whys and wherefores of brain function. We now know that the brain has specific, different physical locations for dealing with emotion and with cognitive rational thinking. These disparate physical locations are interconnected, but often act on their own. We now know how the brain routes information to these areas to make decisions. Most important, we know with greater certainty how to use this information to persuade and influence others.

NEW SCIENTIFIC DISCIPLINES

These functional brain-imaging techniques require both the acquisition of data and the processing of acquired data. Interpreting this data requires a multidisciplinary team of scientists—scientists with disciplines never before imagined. This requirement has created a plethora of new scientific disciplines that could not exist without the new technologies.

We now have almost 20 new scientific disciplines working on real-time brain function and its application to our thinking, to our decision making and actions. These new disciplines include MRI physiology, neurochemistry, neurophysiology, molecular neurobiology, neuroradiology, computational neuroscience, psychophysics, neuropsychology, cognitive neuroscience, and more. The burgeoning list continues to grow and the research of these nascent disciplines provides new information about how we truly react to stimuli—including suggestions and requests from other people. Significantly, it tells us how others react to attempts at persuasion, compliance, and decision making. The guessing—the hit-or-miss shotgun approach to understanding influence and persuasion—is forever changed.

IS THERE REALLY A BREAKTHROUGH?

The new discoveries are spellbinding. For millennia, the rationalists, the behaviorists, and psychologists dating back to Aristotle and

Plato and continuing through the mid-1990s had it wrong. Until recently we thought the higher forms of mental activity—including rationality, cognitive thinking, foresight, and decisions—were based primarily on our use of logic and reason. That's not to say that we always *used* logic and reason but at least in educated circles we generally regarded emotion as an impediment to logic and reason. We believed emotion plays havoc on rationality. Faced with an important decision, we want to remain "reasonable and rational." Yet the fundamental goal of even recent psychology was to reduce the influence and subjectivity of emotion on decision making, actions, and behaviors. With our new window into how the brain processes information, we've learned much about our prior knowledge. We've learned that we had it all backward!

Based on his cutting-edge research, Dr. Richard Restak's book *The Secret Life of the Brain* is a bombshell. The research and the book were so revealing, so startling, that it was made into a five-part PBS television series. The segment, "The Adult Brain," subtitled "To Think by Feeling," provides remarkable new insight into how the brain functions in decision making and in response to persuasion stimuli. The first part tells us, "Adulthood is supposed to correspond to the period in our lives when reason rather than emotion rules." So strong is this emphasis that our entire legal system is based on it. "What would the reasonable man or woman do under such circumstances?"

We tolerantly accept that the actions of kids and teens are too frequently governed by feelings about speeding, drinking, and the like. But adults are expected to act and react reasonably, logically. Ironically, a most interesting revelation is that many things that we logically believe "stand to reason" are actually based on assumptions and experiences having more to do with emotions than reason.

Yet, as Restak explains, "We always react emotionally to even the most trivial of happenings. Without emotions to guide us, we would be incapable of either decisions or plans." From actually seeing live brain function we understand why Restak summarizes human nature stating again, "We are not thinking machines. We are feeling machines that think!"

OLD IDEAS DIE HARD

Wow! For thousands of years we believed the best approach to influence another was with reason and logic. We had been told that emotion inhibits good decisions; but, as noted, new scientific discoveries now tell us, "No way!" Emotions not only guide our decisions and actions but without them we'd be incapable of making decisions. And to persuade effectively, we have to direct our primary stimulus to impact that "Feeling Machine"! Old ideas die hard, yet we must accept that in the real world of decision making, logic and reason alone don't cut it—they have their place, but not the place we once thought.

This concept is so relatively new—so different from what we've been taught, from what we believe—that it is questioned by many. Some will not readily believe it and will follow antiquated dogma. Should you believe it? A broad range of worldwide independent neuroscience research reinforces Restak's findings.

For example, Canadian researcher Dr. Peter Shizgal writes that in contrast to how we perceive the rational, thinking, cognitive pathways of the brain, "The evaluative channel operates without even a pretense of objectivity!"

Commenting on the relationship between rational, logical cognition and emotion, Theodore Roethke states: "We think by feeling." This is a huge departure from the old belief that we think and act with rational cognition and that feelings get in the way.

To understand how we "think by feeling" we need to understand the part of the brain that receives stimuli, emotionally feels what's right, then triggers a response. This brain structure is called the amygdala (a-mig' da-la), an almond-shaped mass of gray matter residing in the brain's temporal lobe. The amygdala is the receptor for virtually all stimuli reaching the brain. It has the option for making its own "feeling" decisions and actions, or it can send the information to the cerebral cortex where evaluative rational thinking is processed.

Today's scientific breakthrough is that, for the first time in mankind's history, we can actually watch in real time the oxygen, blood, and neuron flows in the brain. We can see the amygdala act as the gatekeeper for the thinking part of the brain, the cerebral cortex. We can observe the amygdala trigger immediate emotion-based decisions saving the cerebral cortex from the hard work of evaluative rational thought.

This new knowledge of the amygdala's dynamic role in decision making and resultant actions forms the breakthrough in how we persuade others.

Other researchers have now come on board with even stronger documentation about emotion and intellect. In their work, *Primal Leadership*, Daniel Goleman, Richard Boyatzis, and Annie McKee state, "Although our business culture places great value in an intellect devoid of emotion, our emotions are more powerful than our intellect."

The authors add, "The thinking brain evolved from the limbic brain and continues to take orders from it. The trigger point is the amygdala, a limbic brain structure that scans what's happening to us moment by moment. It commandeers other parts of the brain, including the rational centers of the cortex." Since we've scientifically documented that the amygdala "commandeers other parts of the brain, including the rational centers," doesn't this tell us that we must learn to address our requests to the amygdala rather than to the brain's rational centers? When input to the amygdala triggers the internal emotional navigation system into action, there is no need to send the input to the evaluative center, the cerebral cortex.

Dr. Dean Shibata conducted in vivo brain imaging technology research at the University of Rochester School of Medicine. Shibata found that "when people make decisions that affect their own lives, they will use the emotional parts of the brain even though the task itself may not seem emotional." Our "rational" decisions are more biased than we think. Shibata notes, "There is an increasingly accepted school of thought in neuropsychology that there is a significant emotional component to all personal decision making, and the brain scans in our study support that hypothesis. If you eliminate the emotional guiding factors, it's impossible to make decisions in daily life." The documentation for the validity of the power of emotion over logic now seems irrefutable.

This is heady stuff! It tells us that our prior approaches to gaining compliance from others—to providing the right kind of information to help them make decisions—has to be updated. Significantly, the new research not only corrects our misconceptions about the priority of logic but points the way to how we can benefit from knowing what stimuli to apply to create desired decisions.

In a second study, Shibata discovered that people use the emotional parts of the brain to make what they believe to be rational decisions. He found that the emotional context helps you make the best choice, often in a split second—long before the rational centers of the brain seem able to come into play. Researchers recently made another stunning discovery. When the emotional center of the brain, the amygdala, is damaged, people are incapable of making most decisions, even though their rational brain sites are fully functional.

Because these findings are so new, most of us still believe the use of logic, reason, and a well-prepared rational approach will get

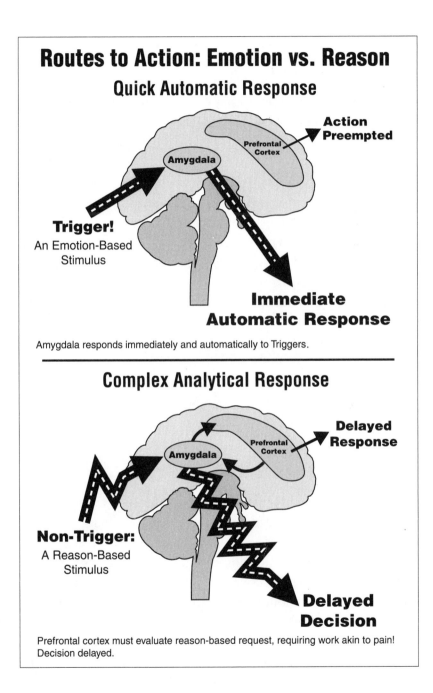

Routes to Action: Emotion vs. Reason
Quick Automatic Response

Action
Preempted

Prefrontal
Cortex

Amygdala

Trigger!
An Emotion-Based
Stimulus

**Immediate
Automatic Response**

Amygdala responds immediately and automatically to Triggers.

Complex Analytical Response

**Delayed
Response**

Prefrontal
Cortex

Amygdala

Non-Trigger:
A Reason-Based
Stimulus

**Delayed
Decision**

Prefrontal cortex must evaluate reason-based request, requiring work akin to pain!
Decision delayed.

people to understand, then comply with our wishes. No wonder we often say in frustration, "He just doesn't get it!" And of course it's not "his" fault—it's ours. Using reason and logic to persuade, we're working against the realities we've recently discovered. We're fighting the brain in a losing battle. The good news is that with this counterintuitive approach, you will have a huge advantage over those who have not yet learned these truths.

The obvious conclusions to be drawn from this research turn much of our current approach to managing and leading people upside down. The findings forever change the realities of management and leadership. Why? Because we can't lead until we can get others to follow. And only with the right tools and approaches, and emotional involvement, can we effectively influence others to comply, to follow, to willingly act, to execute our goals and strategies.

REVIEW AND REFERENCE

- The late 1990s brought a virtual explosion in brain-research capabilities. The combination of new technology, computers, and scientific disciplines has enabled us to finally see live brain functioning. We can see in real time the decision process unfold as the blood, chemical, and neuron flows "light up" specific areas of the brain.

- We can now objectively study the brain functions that generate our moods, thoughts, decisions, and actions. Learning how stimuli can affect our everyday lives, we can finally learn the best ways to guide our partner's decision-making process to help him make desired decisions and actions.

- Until recently we thought the higher forms of mental activity—including rationality, cognitive thinking, and decision making—were based on our use of logic and reason. We believed that emotion plays havoc on rationality. With our new window into how the brain processes information, we've learned that we had it all backward.

- Emotions not only guide our decisions and actions; without emotions we are incapable of making decisions.
- People use the emotional parts of their brains to make what they consider rational decisions. Emotional context helps you make the best choice, often in a split second—long before the rational centers of the brain are activated. Therefore, we must learn to primarily address our requests to the emotional part of the brain rather than to the brain's rational centers.
- The brain structure that receives stimuli, emotionally feels what's right, then triggers a response is called the amygdala. The amygdala is the receptor for virtually all stimuli reaching the brain. It has the option for making its own "feeling" decisions and actions, or it can send the information to the cerebral cortex for laborious rational evaluation.
- Old ideas die hard, but we must accept that in the real world of decision making, logic and reason alone aren't enough. The have their place, but it's not the place we once thought.
- For your CPO, current persuasion opportunity, we have an interactive form to help determine the most persuasive elements for your current persuasion goals. Go to www.seventriggers.com where you can select the applicable elements, make notes, print them out.

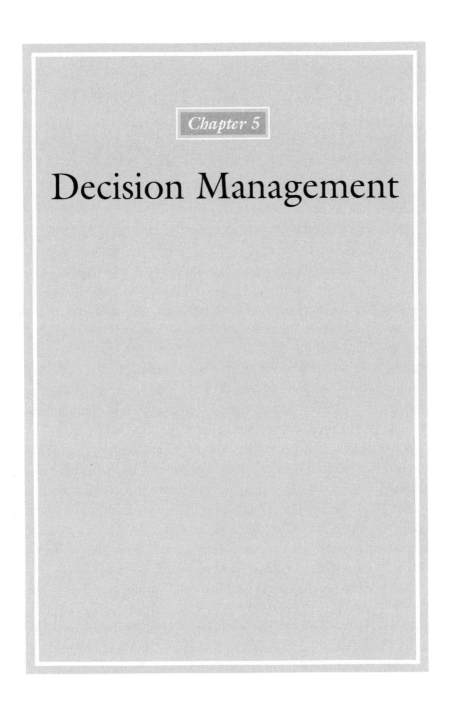

Chapter 5

Decision Management

et's revisit some old concepts regarding the human mind. Until recently we believed there was an executive management center in our mind, in our brain, that controlled our thoughts, decisions, and actions. This concept of an executive control center was often referred to as "the will." Since psychologists and philosophers in the past had no knowledge of brain function, they conjured up the will as the control center of the body and mind. They concluded that we could employ the will to direct our thoughts and actions. The belief was that by using the power of rationality and enforcing rationality with willpower we could make a decision, select choices, decide on a plan of action, comply, or not comply with others' wishes. With a powerful will we could make things happen.

Robert Collier, owner of the early-twentieth-century publishing empire that created *Collier's Encyclopedia* and the nationally distributed *Collier's Weekly* magazine, published a best seller on this topic: *The Power of Will*. The book sold hundreds of thousands of copies in the 1920s. Why? Because we fervently believed that the will controls our thinking and our actions. And the populace wanted better ways to enhance and to benefit from willpower.

As a college psychology major, this concept intrigued me. I ultimately purchased the copyright to this work from the Collier heirs. I tried to fashion my life and my business dealings on the concept of will. Until now, I never understood why it didn't work very well. With the new discoveries in neuroscience, I finally learned that "the will," as we envisioned it, is subservient to the amygdala. The book and the copyright are now archival mementos of an era long past.

Dr. David C. Noelle, professor of psychology and computer science at Vanderbilt University, writes in his article "Exorcizing the Homunculous," "Unfortunately asserting that such a will is the source of our actions does little to advance our understanding, it merely introduces a regress concerning the locus of decision making. It is a truly useless hypothetical construct that explains nothing about the origin of our actions. If we are to understand our own behavior, the will must be exorcised from our mind."

"That exorcism," Noelle adds, "is now under way using the tools of modern experimental psychology and cognitive neuroscience."

The pivotal comment here is "a regress concerning the locus of decision making." We must exorcise old ways and redirect our leadership and persuasion efforts to the true locus of decision making. As the new tools of neuroscience are telling us, "Our thoughtful decisions, our overt words and deeds appear to be produced automatically, without deliberation. . . . In the midst of such automatic behaviors, decisions seem to be made for us, enacted by reflexes and learned habits."

We have only now learned that the locus of decision making is directed by the amygdala.

REAL PERSUASION GOES BEYOND "HIT AND MISS"

So we've learned that our decisions and actions are based on emotional rather than rational responses to stimuli. Haven't advertisers, marketers—yes, even salespeople—known this for years? Haven't these people been learning how to motivate our responses to their ads and presentations? Haven't the great persuaders—the Gateses, the Trumps, and the like—been using this knowledge? Of course they have! But their application of emotional appeals has been, as we've seen, a hit-or-miss, trial-and-error approach. The advertisers, marketers, and others have learned what works, but only through exhaustive experimentation. They have written and re-written billions of words of ad and letter copy, then measured the results to learn what works and what doesn't.

Of course this trial-and-error approach, a laborious and inefficient guesswork process, yielded nothing about *how* or *why* certain appeals work—or don't! They just did or didn't. This random process follows the antiquated behaviorist tradition of attempting to evaluate consequences without understanding the causal relationships.

But what about the naturals, the Trumps, Gateses, the Iacoccas, and the Welches? Well, they have an innate, very rare understanding of human nature. They have a sense for how we make decisions and what motivates us to act. Maybe that's why they're rich and others are not!

NEW DAY BRINGS POWERFUL NEW RESULTS

It's a new day for advertisers, marketers, salespeople, leaders, managers, and, well, anyone who works with others. With our updated knowledge of how the brain actually functions, we can learn how to make presentations that really work—presentations that trigger the inner self-guidance systems in our partners. Is this new day here yet? Can we count on the positive results this new information can bring? Bet on it!

The advertising world is already embarking on applications for the current research tools. And the results are amazing. One discipline well under way is imaging of the brain for detection of visual scene encoding for long-term memory with TV and web commercials. Print commercial evaluations are in the incipient stages. Using SSPT imaging, scientists are learning which visual video images are better recognized, which images are recognized quickest, and which are remembered longest. They have learned that the images that go to the brain's creative and emotional left hemisphere are longest remembered and have the best recall. Previous, erroneous thinking was that images that went to the logic- and data-oriented right hemisphere were best remembered and recalled.

Advertisers are learning that memory retention of specific elements of the ad influences brand awareness and buying behavior. The ad people now can tell even which specific frames in a video ad are more effective. They know, for example, that scenes of 1.5 seconds are more memorable than shorter or longer scenes. The specific visual pictures of cortical activity and the location of image pathways enable advertisers to design commercials with high impact and longer recall. In short, the marketers are putting the new technology to good use in designing ads that work more effectively.

This predictive ability will change the approach to most advertising. The interesting difference between this new scientific approach and the old approaches is that we no longer have to rely on "self-reports." Before the new technology, many facets of marketing, advertising, sales, and yes, *persuasion,* were based on focus-group-type activities. These self-report functions were often in direct opposition to how we actually responded to a real-life similar situation. The new science is demonstrating that we really do not know consciously how our subconscious brain is functioning. We tend to prejudge things, and we have finally learned that our judgment is largely determined by our emotional response.

A simple example is the Pepsi, or Coke challenge. When tests are blind, Pepsi and Coke usually come out even, around 50–50. When the participants know which is Coke, Coke wins, usually by a 25–75 percent margin with the same group of evaluators who previously scored the 50–50 results. These experiments reinforce the knowledge that our conscious thinking, our awareness, does not always know how our emotional brain elements are processing information.

There are many applications for the new knowledge, and the advertising issues are but a small example.

We now know why *UPI Science News* stated, "Even the most analytical people may rely on emotions to make decisions, no matter how rational that decision may seem."

We haven't been privy to that kind of information before. In fact as recently as the mid-1990s there was no opportunity to learn what we're sharing with you now.

Dr. Kelton Rhodes, adjunct professor at the University of Southern California, wrote, "The scientific renaissance at the beginning of this century de-emphasized the persuasive arts. Since there was no true science of persuasion, it wasn't taught in the modern curricular. It still isn't unless you happen to take an advanced social psychology course in college."

Professor Rhodes wrote this in 1997!

Today, a few short years after the scientific explosion, persuasion is a key subject taught in virtually every major graduate business school. And the teaching is based on the new knowledge of real-time brain function.

A GOLDMINE OF POSSIBILITIES

Dr. Jonathan Cohen, professor of psychology at Princeton, puts the rationale for the current experimentation in persuasion in context in an interview for the *UPI* by Bruce Sylvester: "The basic research represents a beginning and a goldmine of possibilities. It will be helpful to all kinds of researchers who study human behavior for whatever reasons."

Whatever your personal goals, whether to be a better leader, manager, marketer, or simply a better communicator, this new knowledge of the realities of human behavior will help you accomplish your goals. Put simply, this new knowledge is a "goldmine of opportunities . . . for whatever reasons."

A news release from the 87th Scientific Assembly of the Radiological Society of North America, an association of more than 30,000 radiologists and physicists in medicine, is titled: "A Rational Decision? Don't Bet On It."

The lead paragraph asks, "Could it be that there is no such thing as a rational decision when it comes to anything involving yourself?"

Perhaps the best synthesis of these new discoveries is offered by Carnegie-Mellon University researchers Colin Camerer and George Loewenstein who were quoted in an article in *Newsweek* called "Mind Reading" as saying:

"The Platonic metaphor of the mind as a charioteer driving the twin horses of reason and emotion is on the right track—except that cognition is a smart pony, and emotion is a big elephant."

Clearly that big elephant outweighs the pony every time.

We are pushing the wagon uphill with a rope when we attempt to lead, persuade, and gain commitment using primarily logic and reason. Now I don't presume to make you an expert on brain function and anatomy. Yet if you want to create better leadership, management, and persuasive ability, it's important that you have a basic understanding of how your partner's brain processes the information you offer. The more knowledge you have about information processing, the easier it will be for you to communicate effectively. The more aware you are, the more you'll be able to apply the power of rapid cognition to get the decisions and actions you seek. After all, your ability to lead is fully dependent on getting the other person to follow, to comply. And you will only succeed by working with her brain—in concert with it, rather than against it!

Brain function is extremely complex. I'll do my best to simplify the basic brain parts and functions most critical to our goal of effec-

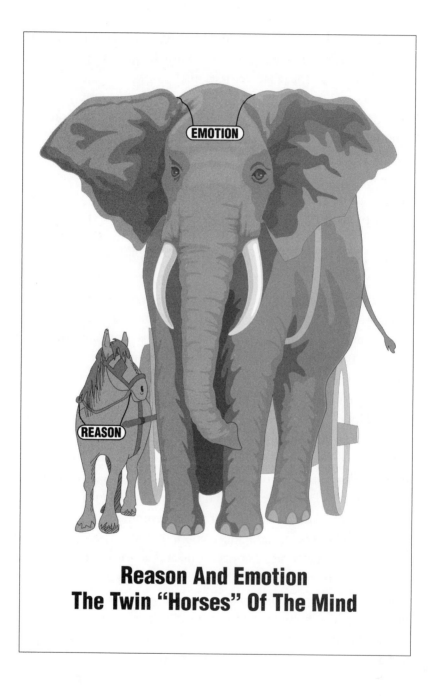

Reason And Emotion
The Twin "Horses" Of The Mind

tive leadership through persuasion. As mentioned in the quote from *Primal Leadership*, the brain's "trigger point for emotional action is the amygdala." The operative word here is "trigger point"; the reason for this will be quickly manifest.

To be effective leaders, managers, marketers, and persuaders we benefit by understanding how two key areas of the brain operate and interact. These are the emotional system and the evaluative, cognitive thinking system. As mentioned previously, we have learned each has separate yet interconnected physical locations in the brain. Researchers tell us "Discrete functions occur in specific locations." The key areas are the amygdala in the emotional limbic system, and the prefrontal cortex where reason and cognitive evaluation take place.

As quoted above, "The trigger point is the amygdala, a limbic brain structure that scans what's happening to us moment by moment." It is part of the ancient limbic system, and the limbic system controls our feelings, our emotions, and our actions. Brain function may seem esoteric, yet understanding how others process information is critical to helping us persuade and influence our persuasion partners.

PERSUASION—TRIGGERED BY THE AMYGDALA

As part of the limbic system, which stores ancient "triggers," the amygdala is one of the very few brain elements functioning at birth. Why are we so dependent—yes, from birth—on the amygdala? Well, if it were not for the amygdala we might not be here. The triggers for "do or don't," "freeze," and "fight or flight" were developed at a time when humans were threatened by hungry lions or bears. In such instances, if we stopped to think of our many options, if we used cognitive thought to logically evaluate the nuances of the situation, if we tarried just a bit, we'd be lunch meat. We would then be unable to pass along our genetic heritage. The amygdala's triggers preserved our lives and our heritage.

The amygdala works tirelessly for us in a vast array of situations. When driving, you might notice the car in front slowing down. Using cognitive thought you can decide to slow down, check the mirror, pull to the left or right, blink your lights, or blow your horn. But if that car makes a sudden stop, the amygdala triggers an immediate reaction—you slam on the brakes. And you do so long before the sensory input even reaches the cognitive areas of the brain.

Not surprisingly, in patients with amygdala damage there are deficits in their startle response to emotional stimuli. When rats have scientifically generated amygdala damage, they will actually cuddle up with cats!

We've learned that the amygdala is working for us from the minute we're born. Yet the rational and cognitive areas in the prefrontal cortex are not fully matured and functional until we are in our mid-twenties! No wonder we are so reliant on the amygdala! No wonder teens do things we shake our heads at. They are for the most part incapable of fully and objectively analyzing the outcomes of smoking, drugs, sex, and risky behavior. The brain hasn't gotten there yet.

Does the brain have tools to generate action without rational, cognitive thought? Scientific evidence more and more supports that concept. Numerous controlled studies offering learning situations confirm that the "automatic" elements of the brain learn "better or worse" choices long before the awareness or cognitive centers pick up the clues.

Joshua Brown, Ph.D., professor in the department of psychological and brain sciences at Indiana University, writes in the journal *Science,* "It appears that the brain is somehow figuring out things without you necessarily having to be consciously aware of it . . . the adjustments may be even more robust when made on a subconscious level."

Susan Phelps, Ph.D., director of the Phelps Lab at NYU's psychology department, states in an interview in *Psychology Today:* "The amygdala has been called the seat of emotion. It can get information about the emotional significance of an event prior to our awareness of it."

And we're learning that the emotional significance is stronger than the logical, rational significance. The amygdala handles the first response to stimuli; and it initiates an emotional, not cognitive response. So we have the amygdala which gets all of the sensory input, sends some of that input to the cognitive, rational centers for evaluation and possible action. Which part of the brain then determines our quick, automatic decisions and actions?

James McGaugh, founding director of the department of psychobiology at the University of California, points up the issue. "You've got a clash between the prefrontal cortex, which is trying to make sense of what's going on at the moment, and the amygdala which instructs the brain to induce emotional arousal."

McGaugh adds the critical element of truth from the new research: "Unfortunately, the amygdala too often trumps the prefrontal cortex in almost all of us."

The amygdala can bypass or overwhelm the prefrontal lobes so that we react without evaluative thinking.

Dr. Joseph LeDoux, neuroscientist at New York University, also contributed to the PBS *The Secret Life of the Brain* series. LeDoux puts the new information in context. "As things now stand, the amygdala has greater influence on the cortex than the cortex has on the amygdala, allowing emotional arousal to dominate and control thinking."

PLAY THE TRUMP CARD

This realization, based on live, real-time brain imaging, puts a whole new light on how we must work with our partner's brain to produce the decisions and results we want. To persuade effectively we need to work with the amygdala—and let it naturally trump the prefrontal cortex! To succeed at persuasion we have to direct our appeals to the center of emotional action, to the amygdala. Let's pull, not push, on the rope to get the wagon uphill.

Everything you do—your thoughts, actions, decisions and behaviors—is dependent on your emotional responses to your prior experience. Each decision you make is prompted by decisions of the past. When faced with making a decision, you call upon past decisions, past precedents to guide the next one. (How about our system of jurisprudence—all based on case precedent.) You call upon an emotional memory that will appear as a gut reaction, a feeling that will guide you in the right direction. This same process impacts your partner's decisions and actions.

The memories stored in the amygdala begin before birth and are indelible, imprinted in your brain for all time. They become your databank, the resources you will draw upon for your entire life. Your brain has stored all of this information to provide you with an internal instantaneous navigational aid system. It is our personal self-guidance system, activated by our own internal triggers. *The Secret Life of the Brain* adds, "So what you have is literally a navigational aid—something that gets you to the right decision. If that is broken down you are at the mercy of facts and logic, and that's just not good enough."

Our internal self-guidance systems and internal triggers allow us to navigate through a lifetime of everyday activities that we could never manage if we had to employ cognitive, rational evaluation for each and every decision and action. Facts and logic are, well, "just not good enough!"

Let's recap the documentation the new technology and the new science have provided for us.

• The amygdala is the emotional trigger point for our decisions and actions.
• From birth, the amygdala builds our internal self-guidance system's database.
• The self-guidance system is activated by our own internal triggers.
• The self-guidance system and its triggers define our decisions and actions.

Conclusion: To effectively lead and achieve results through others, to persuade them to do what is right for us and for them, we must:

• Learn which internal triggers universally motivate the decisions and actions we want.
• Learn which internal triggers will help our partner activate his own self-guidance system.
• Create a presentation that will activate our partner's self-guidance system and trigger a response for a shared, mutually beneficial, positive conclusion.

We're going to show you precisely, in full detail, how to get what you want by effectively employing this science and art. Thanks to today's neuroscientific discoveries, we can now make persuasion as much of a science as it has been an art.

REVIEW AND REFERENCE

• We formerly believed that there was a human executive control center, often referred to as "the will," that controlled our thoughts, decisions, and actions. We now know "the will" is a figment of the imagination of early psychologists who, lacking today's scientific knowledge, created the concept. We also know the control centers are primarily the amygdala and the cerebral cortex.

- The amygdala is the emotional trigger point for our decisions and actions. We base our decisions on emotional rather than rational responses to stimuli.
- We must learn to address our persuasion requests to the amygdala rather than merely the brain's rational centers. Emotions dominate and control thinking. Even analytical people rely on emotions to make decisions.
- Each decision you make is prompted by decisions of the past. Every time you make a decision, you subconsciously call upon an emotional memory that will appear as a gut reaction, a feeling that will guide you in the right direction.
- We each build a database, our personal self-guidance system. To persuade, we must learn to help our partner activate her own self-guidance system. When we activate our partner's amygdala triggers, we preclude time-consuming, painful, laborious thinking.
- For your CPO, current persuasion opportunity, we have an interactive form to help determine the most persuasive elements for your current persuasion goals. Go to www.seventriggers.com where you can select the applicable elements, make notes, and print them out.

Chapter 6

Persuasion Powerhouses

ow do we build persuasive communications? How do we use knowledge of brain processes to significantly influence our partner's self-guidance and internal trigger systems? How do we generate shared solutions that achieve desired conclusions?

RHETORIC AND PERSUASION

Let's scroll back again to the early days of persuasion. In the fourth century BCE, rhetoric grew along with democracy. Aristotle, Plato, and other researchers quickly realized that persuasion was the primary means for succeeding in an era when people were no longer dependent upon the mercy or whims of royal ascendancy or the force of dictatorship.

In his three volumes, Aristotle described rhetoric as "the faculty of observing in any given case the available means of persuasion." Aristotle's research defined the three main elements of every persuasive argument or presentation. As noted earlier, he called these elements *ethos, logos,* and *pathos.* Incredibly prescient, he got the elements right. We recognize that these same three elements control every instance of persuasion today. Only the names have changed for these basic internal triggers.

THE POWERHOUSES OF PERSUASION—ETHOS, LOGOS, PATHOS

Ethos is the credibility, the knowledge, the expertise, and the stature of the speaker. Today we refer to ethos as authority. If you are looked upon as a knowledgeable expert in the context you are dealing with, you are an authority. Establish your authority and you are a step up in the persuasion process.

Logos is the appeal of logic, reason, cognitive thinking, data, and facts. Used properly, and at the right time, logos is critical to persuasion. Today we refer to logos as logic.

Pathos is the appeal to emotions, the noncognitive, nonthinking reasons we make decisions and take action. While pathos was always known to be an element in persuasion, recent neurologic discovery, as we've seen, documents new understandings on the significant role of emotion in decision making and in persuasion. We now refer to pathos as emotion.

Authority, logic, and emotion are the powerhouse building blocks of every persuasive argument or presentation. They are the internal triggers common to any persuasion situation. Let's look at a simple example of these building blocks in action.

You've been having some shortness of breath, and uneasy feelings in the chest area. After much procrastination, you call a cardiologist for an appointment. You've already been persuaded by your internal authority trigger to select a cardiologist over a general practitioner. The ethos for the cardiologist is much higher than that of a GP. How then does the cardiologist enhance the perception of his authority? Does his office wall sport a bevy of plaques and certificates attesting to his training and awards? Is there a Board Certification plaque? A list of hospital connections? Is he wearing typical doctor garb? Does he hang a stethoscope around his neck? There are probably pictures and models of the heart around the room. He's an authority, and displays it. His knowledge, experience, and expertise are important to you, right?

Now for the logos—the logic—the data and the facts. The cardiologist tells you that your HDL (high-density lipoprotein) is 56, your LDL (low-density lipoprotein) is 147, and your total cholesterol is 283. The HDL/LDL ratio is marginal. Your systolic blood pressure is 147, the diastolic pressure is 96, and triglycerides are 209. The cardiologist tells you the data puts your CHD risk factor for potential death by coronary disease at 5.3. The logic cognitively evaluated from this data indicates potential problems.

But are you persuaded to take any action based on authority and facts, data, and logic? Like most of us, can you even make sense of the data—make it meaningful? Or do you wonder, what does all this mean to me?

Let's go for the pathos—the emotional appeal. After reviewing the file, your doctor tells you that you could have a debilitating stroke, a heart attack, even die in the not-too-distant future if you do not make some immediate changes in diet, exercise, stress reduction, and lifestyle. You immediately flash to seeing yourself incapacitated, or your wife and kids without a husband and father. Does this get your attention?

Which appeal is most likely to motivate you to make the requisite changes? Certainly each element—authority, logic of the facts and data, and emotion—combine to play a role in your reaction. Yet the effect of the emotional appeal far outweighs the others. Remember the "smart pony–big elephant" scenario? The emotional elephant always outweighs the smart pony.

MENTAL RESPONSE—AUTOMATIC OR ANALYTICAL?

How do we know which appeal, which internal trigger—authority, logic, or emotion—to use in any given persuasion situation? The answer depends on the thinking mode of our partner. Each of us has different modes of thinking and responding to stimuli.

Ohio State University researchers Richard Petty and John Cacioppo explain the most fundamental difference in receptivity to a persuasion attempt. They state that a person will respond either "centrally or peripherally." New York University's Shelly Chaiken defines the receptivity as either "systematic or heuristic."

In plain English, the scientists have determined that we respond to persuasion attempts either mindfully or mindlessly; analytically or automatically. The analytics, those who respond "mindfully," will carefully and thoughtfully consider the authority of the persuader, then evaluate the rationality, the facts, the logic of the situation or proposal. They will use a reasoned, cognitive, evaluative approach to the facts presented. They will take an alert, active role in the thinking process, using judgment, analysis, concentration, and a strong cognitive effort.

Those who respond "mindlessly," those in the automatic mode, will generate a decision, an attitude change, and an action based on cues or triggers that will help them make easy, nondeliberative, automatic decisions. For those easy choices, they will go with their amygdala-based gut feelings, with their built-in self-guidance system and triggers.

WHO'S IN THE AUTOMATIC MODE?

Great information. But how do we know which mode our partner is in? Fortunately, research provides the answer. As the sum of this research tells us, "all people most of the time, and most people all of the time, are in the automatic mode!" And for those few who are in the mindful, analytical mode, here's the kicker: the information your partner processes does not have to be rational at all; it only has to make sense to that person at that time.

71

Should we doubt these findings about the thinking modes of our partner? Based on the evidence, probably not. Lawyers have documented that "guilty" or "not guilty" trial verdicts are determined fully 80 percent of the time based on jurors' "gut reactions" to just the lawyer and his opening statements! In 80 percent of trials, four out of five guilty decisions are made long before any of the evidence is presented. Yet the only charge the judge gives to a juror is to determine guilt or innocence based on evidence. The jurors' thinking mode is apparent. They're supposed to weigh the evidence. Statistically, they usually don't.

Science finally has learned that our brains simply do not work in the logic mode.

We're always looking for and are influenced by our self-guidance system and its internal triggers. To better understand how to effectively persuade, we'll benefit from knowing why people act as they do. Why they are usually in the automatic mode. This knowledge will help us prepare our persuasive presentations.

TO THINK OR NOT TO THINK?

Why do we seek the easy way out? Why do we seem to avoid the cognitive, rational thought process? Why are we not inclined to employ logic in our decision making? Why do we studiously avoid analysis, evaluation, and cognitive thought? The answer: We avoid cognitive evaluation like the plague—because it's hard work! It takes time and effort. Henry Ford sensed this a hundred years ago when he said, "Thinking is the hardest work there is, which is probably why so few engage in it."

Author James Thurber adds his own comment: "Sixty minutes of thinking of any kind is bound to lead to confusion and unhappiness."

Influence researcher Ellen Langer has coined the term "cognitive misers" to describe us and our decision process. Dr. Gregory

Neidert says we are running our brains at idle 90 to 95 percent of the time.

We know how we act, but why do we act this way? Scientists have evaluated neurologic brain waves to determine the types of waves emitted when the brain is working hard. This activity might include cognitive evaluation functions, say, solving a math problem. Under these conditions, subjects emitted and the scientists captured very distinctive, specific brain waves. But here's the shocker—virtually the same brain waves were evidenced when the subjects plunged their hands and arms into ice water! The human brain has the same response to evaluative, cognitive, logical thinking as it does to the pain of ice water. Thinking is not only hard work, it hurts! It's painful! We just don't like it. So we avoid thinking whenever we can.

Scientists have measured the energy consumption of the brain at different stages of information processing. They have found that the brain consumes about 300 percent more caloric energy when engaged in cognitive evaluation, logical thinking, than when idling in the automatic mode. Bottom line? When you ask your partner to evaluate your well-researched, well-prepared data and logic, your beautifully reasoned logical approach for doing something, you're courting trouble. You're asking him to jump into ice water. You're asking him to spend 300 percent more energy than he wants to. You're asking him to endure pain. Is that smart?

Another road block to persuasion using a rational, logical presentation is comprehension. We often fail to persuade with a rational presentation simply because the partner just doesn't get it. Faced with a bevy of data, facts, and figures, with reams of information, the partner has to work too hard to understand, to fully comprehend where you're going. He will not analytically process the information but will instead revert to the easy thinking automatic mode. Don't confuse me with the facts!

What then is the secret to efficient persuasion? It's simply to recognize that your partner is most likely to be in the automatic thinking mode. Knowing this, you can now evaluate which internal triggers she will most likely employ to motivate the decision and action you seek.

How do you determine your partner's mode and tolerance for a rational, reasoned approach? I've given you one clue. As mentioned previously, all people most of the time and most people all of the time are in the automatic mode.

There are of course exceptions. CPAs, lawyers, doctors, engineers, economists, and the like are generally open to a more detailed, facts-and-figures, more reasoned, logos approach. But don't count on it. Even these people rely on the emotional, amygdala response.

In a recent *Newsweek* article, "The New Science of Decision Making," Jacqueline Bohnert writes, "For all its intellectual power and success as a creator of wealth, free-market economics rests on a fallacy. This is the belief that people apply rational calculations to economic decisions. The world doesn't actually work this way." Even the number crunchers can be swayed more by the amygdala—the emotional motivator.

We are bored and short-tempered with data, facts, and figures. Professor Richard Boyatzis at Case Western University states in an interview with Betty A. Martin for *Harvard Management Communication Letter,* "You don't excite people by giving them factual answers." Remember the cardiologist example?

MAKE IT EASY

So make persuasion easy! When you want to create change, or motivate action, recognize that most of us do not act on reason and logic. Even if the data create interest, it takes emotion to motivate action.

People do what they want—what is comfortable for them based on their own built-in self-guidance system and internal triggers. Make persuasion easy by helping people see that your proposal, your request, is in concert with their own guidance systems. Help them be consistent with their past actions and thoughts. With the right appeal, they will make a "gut reaction" that will work for both of you.

As mentioned, I run a training company and in our training courses we ask people what kind of watch they are wearing. Is it analog or digital? Timex or Rolex? Sport or dress? Round face, square, oval, or oblong? White face? Black face? Ordinal numbers, Roman numbers, dots, or no numbers? Metal band? Gold, silver, black? Leather band? Brown, black? And on it goes. The ostensible reason—the logical reason—we bought the watch is to tell time. But we bought the specific watch we're wearing on an emotional impulse—we liked it! It exemplified our "style." It reinforced our concept of self.

How might you persuade someone to buy one of the many watches on the market? With logic—telling them how well it keeps time—or by questioning, to learn what drives their watch-buying emotion? The interesting issue here is the obvious element emotion plays. Logically, the Timex keeps time as well as the Rolex. If we bought on logic, few would buy the Rolex; yet the Rollie has huge worldwide sales based on the emotions related to status, accomplishment, success, and vanity. Remember this example—it informs every persuasion attempt you encounter.

Does logic or reason play a role, even with the knowledge that most of us most of the time are in the automatic mode? Of course it does. We make decisions based on emotion, then justify those decisions with logic and reason. We buy the car because we like it—the ride, the look, the feel, maybe even the sales rep. Then we justify the decision with logic. The good gas mileage, the extended warranty, the consumer reports, the side airbags, etc.

And it's the logic we tell our friends and neighbors about. Then we ultimately believe logic was the motivator. Don't we love to fool ourselves?

Logic is an important element in the final persuasion process. Yet logic will almost never persuade change or motivate action. Your persuasion goal is to motivate action through emotional internal triggers, then provide the logical backup justification for the decision. Until now, most of us have conducted the process backwards. Hopefully you'll never again miss a persuasion opportunity with a backward approach.

Skilled persuaders help their partners make decisions that are "shared conclusions." The persuader learns what the partner values, hopes for, what he has done before, and then does the heavy thinking for the partner. They then motivate action with the appropriate internal triggers.

The correct preparation and application of the three main triggers—authority, logic, and emotion—will make a huge difference in your persuasion efforts. Next we will look more closely at how these triggers work, then provide several additional triggers that produce the results we seek. We'll show you how to determine which triggers to use, and when to use them.

REVIEW AND REFERENCE

- Aristotle defined three main elements of every persuasive argument or presentation. We still recognize that these three elements control every instance of persuasion.
- *Ethos* is the credibility, the knowledge, the expertise, the stature, and the authority of the speaker. We refer to ethos as authority. Establish your authority and you are a step up in the persuasion process.

- *Logos* is the appeal of logic, reason, cognitive thinking, data, and facts. Used properly, logos is important to persuasion. Today we refer to logos as logic.

- *Pathos* is the appeal to emotions, the noncognitive, nonthinking motivations when we make decisions and take action. We now refer to pathos as emotion.

- Authority, logic, and emotion are the powerhouse building blocks of every persuasive argument or presentation. They are the macro internal triggers common to any persuasion situation.

- We respond to persuasion attempts either analytically or automatically. Those who respond analytically will use the reasoned, evaluative approach to come to a decision.

- Those who respond automatically will use their self-guidance system to generate a decision. Internal emotional triggers will help them make easy, nondeliberative, automatic decisions.

- All people most of the time, and most people all of the time, are in automatic mode! We avoid cognitive evaluation because it's hard work. The human brain has the same response to evaluative, cognitive, logical thinking as it does to pain.

- Most people do not act on logic and reason. We make emotional decisions, then justify with logic and reason.

- For your CPO, current persuasion opportunity, we have an interactive form to help determine the most persuasive elements for your current persuasion goals. Go to www.seventriggers.com where you can select the applicable elements, make notes, and print them out.

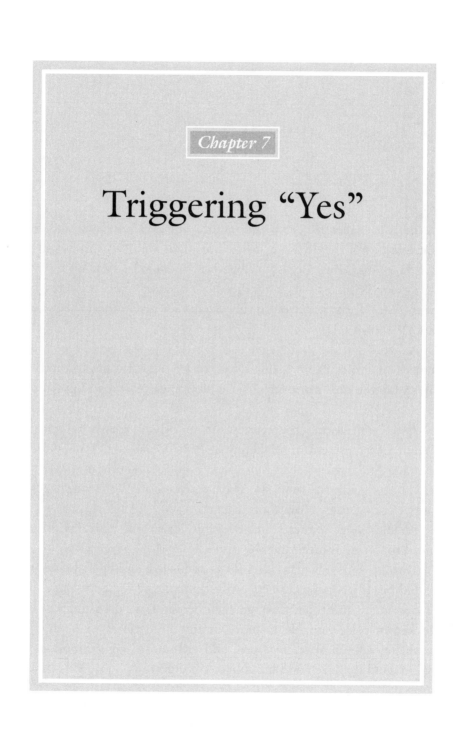

Chapter 7

Triggering "Yes"

ife is a challenge. From the minute our eyes pop open in the morning until they close exhausted at night we deal with an avalanche of decisions. Get out of bed now or snooze? What to wear? What for breakfast—stick to the diet or enjoy? Which route to work? Stop for gas now or on the way home? Listen to the news or a CD? Which CD?

At work it's the same—get that report out first or answer the emails and voice mail? Take my calls or let the voice mail pick up? What are the boss's priorities? What are mine? Whose do I execute first?

And don't forget the requests from others. Dawn Hudson, senior vice-president of marketing at Pepsi-Cola, says, "Today the average American receives more than 3,000 marketing messages a day!" The family has requests. The boss has more. Your staff needs answers, decisions. How about clients?

All day long, requests and decisions drive our activities. The need to decide is incessant; the issues never stop, never let up.

Dealing with this many decisions sounds like an impossibility. It could be. If we had to use cognitive thinking, if we had to *rationally* evaluate and think through each decision, we'd be trapped—locked in place—unable to move in any direction as we analyze, evaluate, contemplate, measure, and critique all of the options. We'd wind up dazed and immobile. We'd go nuts!

NATURE'S TRIGGERS TO THE RESCUE

Fortunately, nature, our limbic system, has provided us with a highly effective, simple solution to enable us to easily get through each decision-making opportunity. That solution is the "navigation system" referred to in *The Secret Life of the Brain,* the system facilitated by our amygdala and activated by our personal databank of internal triggers.

The secret for persuasion success is to find out how people employ their own personalized internal triggers to avoid total analysis paralysis. Often we rely on a single piece of relevant information, a shortcut, to guide us to the right decision. A knowledgeable persuader will learn how a single trigger will motivate the action he seeks. The weird irony of this need for quick, easy triggers is that the more sophisticated and complex our lives get, the more information we have, the more we need and rely on simple ways to help us make decisions and get through each day. Smart managers, leaders, and marketers understand this need and prepare their requests accordingly.

Do we all have this capacity to make quick decisions based on our internal triggers? *Blink,* the book by Malcolm Gladwell, was at the top of the *New York Times* and other best-seller lists for months. Gladwell refers to this ability to make rapid nonthinking decisions as "thin slicing." Thin slicing refers to rapid cognition, automated, accelerated, unconscious solutions to complex situations. Gladwell states, "Thin slicing refers to the ability of our unconscious to find patterns in situations and behavior based on very narrow slices of experience. The power of knowing, in that first two seconds is not a gift given to a fortunate few." We each have that power. It's our internal guidance system. We'd be lost without it.

Gladwell adds, "Snap judgments take place behind closed doors—they suggest that what we think of as 'free will' is largely an illusion: much of the time we are on automatic pilot."

We've all watched thin slicing, snap judgments, and quick decisions in action. Gladwell tells about a purchase of a sixth-century statue by the Getty Museum. Careful cognitive analysis proved the statue to be authentic. The factual research—including the fact that the statue's patina could only have developed over thousands of years—was documented in *Scientific American*. After the purchase, others looked at the statue and in a "blink"—in literally two seconds—they *felt* something was wrong. They were right; the statue was a fake. The patina on the marble was developed in just months, using potato mold. While cognitive research proved it was real, gut feelings proved otherwise.

Gladwell tells another story about tennis star and coach Vic Braden. Braden could tell with 100 percent accuracy when a tournament player will double fault on a second serve. How does Braden do this? He hasn't got a clue. The answer is hidden in his databank.

Many years ago I enjoyed the company of "The Deacon," Arnold Palmer's father and teacher, following Arnold during a PGA tournament round. Arnold's dad would tell me with unerring accuracy precisely where Arnold's ball would land immediately as the ball was struck. When I asked him how he did this, how he knew, he answered, "I don't know," then offered "maybe the shoulders?" He was thin slicing from the internal databank he had assembled over the years of watching Arnold play.

My wife Janet is a super thin slicer. While I wrestle with the pros and cons, the merits of a new acquaintance, Janet has made up her mind in, well, a blink! And she's usually right on target! Your partner will *thin slice* like everyone else. We just have to activate those "narrow slices," those internal triggers to motivate the decisions we want.

At Arizona State University, Dr. Robert Cialdini puts the process into easy perspective. Cialdini's research, revealed in his best-selling book *Influence,* discovered that we respond to "a distinct kind of automatic, mindless compliance, a willingness to say 'yes' without thinking first." Cialdini adds a very valuable suggestion, "It will be increasingly important for society to understand the how and why of automatic influence." I will do my best to help you win by learning the how and the why.

ACTIVATING AUTOMATIC DECISIONS

How do we generate automatic influence? With triggers. Your partner's internal triggers. His personal database that helps him navigate to successful conclusions.

We've talked about our self-guidance navigation system and its functional tools, triggers, which activate our partner's decisions and actions. But what is a trigger? What is this powerful tool that initiates "automatic, mindless compliance"? A trigger is any stimulus that will help us make an automatic, nonthinking decision or action. A trigger activates the receiver's immediate response to the persuader's influence attempt. We, each and every one of us, are pre-programmed to comply with requests when the request activates the appropriate triggers. A trigger is a shortcut to avoid the pain of mental activity, of laborious cognitive rational evaluation.

When a veteran hands us a paper poppy, it triggers an automatic response—we part with a buck. A reasonable request from a trusted friend triggers a positive response. When our kids need new sneakers, they check what their peers are wearing and automatically pick that brand. Conformity is a quick, nonthinking trigger.

Triggers, like memories in the amygdala, are indelible; we never forget them. The lesson? Go with the learned database, don't fight it! It's easier, and more comfortable to go with our partner's own tried, tested triggers.

There are an infinite number of triggers to motivate action in ourselves and others. Consciously or not, you've been using them to some degree in your attempts to persuade others. We are now going to provide you with a system, a process to help you become consciously competent at motivating another's internal triggers to achieve the desired and hopefully mutual goals. No longer will you ask your partner to waste an extra 300 percent effort to weigh a lot of data and information. No longer will you create mental pain similar to putting his hands into ice water.

Research has uncovered the "super seven" triggers that we universally employ to help us make quick, easy, nonthinking decisions. The triggers reside in the other person, and when properly activated, will create automatic compliance. These seven triggers powerfully impact every level of communication, every interaction we have with others. Whether you are sending an email, a letter, creating an advertisement, speaking before a group, or conducting a one-on-one chat, the right triggers will save time, effort, energy, and resources. They can produce the results you want.

For the first time we can apply these triggers in a well-framed, powerful presentation that we know can motivate action by working with the brain's natural process. We now know how and why the brain responds as it does to certain stimuli. You can ignore these new scientific findings. You can deny these triggers exist. And yes, it will be hard for some to embrace the newly documented scientific realities. But embrace these findings and you'll be a more effective persuader.

Those who embrace this knowledge, who learn to motivate the right internal triggers, have enormous power over others. They motivate change. They get approvals for new ideas, get funding for projects. They get cooperation. They get people to say, "Yes!" And, as leaders, they get willing compliance and desired results with others.

There are of course an infinite number of triggers that form our internal self-guidance systems. We each create triggers to help us get to the best quick, easy decisions. We have ascertained the seven important triggers employed by virtually everyone:

1. Friendship
2. Authority
3. Consistency
4. Reciprocity
5. Contrast
6. Reason why
7. Hope

Thanks to new discoveries in live brain function we finally understand how we employ and benefit from our internal guidance systems, our triggers. Triggers work for us because we are—as the scientific evidence now clearly reveals—"feeling machines that think; not thinking machines that feel," as Restak stated. A trigger helps us quickly sense and feel what makes a good decision or action. Our triggers help us navigate paths that would be overwhelming and totally unmanageable if we had to constantly employ cognitive thought. As *The Secret Life of the Brain* states, without these "feelings," these navigation tools, we would be dependent on logic. *And that's just not good enough.* Our triggers are our answer to getting to the right decisions. We can employ these triggers individually, in sequence, or they can be combined for best effect.

WHY SEVEN TRIGGERS?

Why learn seven triggers? Many of us already understand and employ one trigger, the "needs/benefit" approach to gaining compliance. The old idea of "find a need and fill it." But this is only one element of only one trigger, the *hope* trigger. Applying only this approach, we are a one-trick pony. This approach is very limiting. Why use just one element of persuasion when you can dynamically enhance your success ratio by tapping into several internal triggers? We now have powerful tools to multiply our success ratio by a factor of seven or more.

In the following chapters, I'll explain each trigger, share how each works, and provide examples of the trigger in action. For each trigger, I'll provide a list of "trigger elements," specific items you will consider to help plan and execute each trigger. After the seven triggers are explained, I'll provide the process for framing, delivering, and executing your persuasive communication.

Do you have a real-world CPO? A Current Persuasion Opportunity? Something you'd love to get someone to say "Yes" to? To decide and act upon? To help you get the most from each trigger, why not list the applicable elements of each trigger to your CPO? Give this a try—when you complete the book, you'll hit the street running, you'll achieve your YES!

Dig in—enjoy the triggers, add your own thoughts to ours. I believe these triggers will change your life. Let's start with the first.

REVIEW AND REFERENCE

- The need to make decisions never stops. It's impossible to rationally evaluate and think through each of the many daily decisions we make—we'd be locked in place—unable to move as we analyze, evaluate, contemplate, measure, and critique all the options.
- Nature has provided us with a highly effective simple solution to enable us to easily get through each decision-making opportunity. The solution is our navigation system, facilitated by our amygdala and personal databank of internal triggers.
- The secret of persuasion is to find out how people employ their own personalized internal triggers to avoid total analysis paralysis.

- We use "thin slicing" to make rapid nonthinking decisions. We all have this capacity to make quick decisions based on our internal triggers.
- Triggers reside in our internal databank and help us make automatic, nonthinking decisions or actions. A trigger is a shortcut we employ to avoid the pain of heavy mental lifting, of laborious cognitive rational evaluation.
- Working with just "find a need and fill it" is a one-trick-pony approach. Leverage your results by activating multiple triggers.
- There are an infinite number of triggers to motivate action. We create our own triggers to help us get to the best quick, easy decisions. We have researched and defined the seven most important triggers that universally benefit everyone.
- For your CPO, current persuasion opportunity, we have an interactive form to help determine the most persuasive elements for your current persuasion goals. Go to www.seventriggers.com where you can select the applicable elements, make notes, and print them out.

Chapter 8

Friendship Trigger

W ant easy compliance from others? Be well liked. Be a friend. Be trusted.

Getting people to do what you want is easy when people like you, when you are considered a friend. Friendship, liking, is one of the most powerful triggers in the persuasion galaxy. Friendship generates trust, and trust activates a strong internal trigger. The *friendship trigger* encompasses all elements that create positive feelings in others—likeability, trust, similar interests, dependability, fairness, compatibility, cooperation, teamwork, collaboration—the list is endless.

Friendship is perhaps our most important trigger. Liking is a prerequisite for most other triggers to be effective. Be a friend and the other triggers will work well. Miss out on liking and friendship, be disliked, and virtually nothing else will work.

WIN YOUR PARTNER'S TRUST WITH BONDING

Why is friendship such a powerful internal trigger? The amygdala has been storing data in this trigger since the moment of birth. Bonding creates liking and trust. Every animal, including humans, begins the bonding process at birth. We bond with whoever initially cares for us. Cats, dogs, and other pets bond with human "parents." We bond with aunts, uncles, and surrogate parents. In a short time, the amygdala is indelibly hardwired to respond to the trigger of liking and trusting. The data for that indelible trigger grows for a lifetime.

We need to add one more element to the trigger of friendship: trust. Honesty is an element of trust, and an important part of the friendship trigger. Be honest in all of your dealings and in your persuasion presentations. People like and trust you more if they know you're honest.

There's a wealth of research documenting the power of the friendship trigger. Today we know how the circuitry works to trigger a positive friendship response. If you're not a friend, become one. If you can't become a friend, at least be well liked. Be honest and credible, do whatever it takes to become liked. Be a friend and you will more easily gain compliance.

LIKING IS CRITICAL

Before we were aware of how the brain processed decision information, we used a hit-or-miss approach to the friendship trigger. We tried an approach; if it worked, we continued to use it. Lawyers have been using this hit-or-miss system for ages, but now for the first time they know how and why it works. They can now plan accordingly.

Based on accumulated knowledge, lawyers knew that for some reason liking was critical to a jury. If they could get the jury to like their client, they had a much better chance to obtain the desired verdict. The same is invariably true for the lawyer—if the jury likes the lawyer, facts and logic take a back seat. Remember the statistic about verdicts, that 80 percent are based on the lawyer's opening statement, a significant part of which is that lawyer's likeability.

Fundraising organizations have, through trial and error, learned that friendship, liking, and trust play a big part in persuading people to donate to their cause. How do they employ the friendship trigger? By getting local people to solicit from their friends and neighbors. I couldn't begin to count how many times my wife was tapped by various charities to call on neighbors, friends, and relatives to raise funds for national charities. She was far more successful than an outsider would have been.

Virtually every multilevel marketing program employs the friendship trigger. Home party companies get women to bring their friends into their own homes for a friendly "demonstration." The sales pitch becomes a social evening with trusted friends. They buy. Then they form endless chains of sellers and buyers.

Documented analyses of medical malpractice lawsuits reinforce the friendship trigger. In the majority of suits the doctors were not sued primarily because of bad medicine; they were sued because of the way the patients felt they were treated on a personal level. In addition to a medical problem the litigants felt the doctor didn't respect them, rushed them through, belittled them, were hostile or aloof. Put simply, doctors who are well liked are less likely to get sued.

How about politics? Liking is the biggest trigger for voters. Ronald Reagan wasn't the quintessential administrator but he was well liked. He was a friend. He was reelected by the biggest landslide ever. Clinton was a lightning rod on some issues, but even his enemies liked him. He got reelected easily.

George W. Bush probably made more mistakes than many of his predecessors. John Kerry had the opportunity of a lifetime. Kerry was ahead in the polling ratings on virtually every issue prior to the 2004 election. Chris Matthews, host of NBC's *Hardball* put Kerry's problem in succinct context during an interview on the Washington affiliate of CBS. In the preelection interview, Matthews said there was a surprising disconnect between the ratings on the issues and the candidate's overall polling figures. When asked why, Matthews responded: "They just don't like Kerry." The results proved Matthews right.

But here's the interesting element—most voters didn't like Bush either; they simply disliked Kerry more. Be advised! Dislike and distrust are strong motivators.

We vote and are persuaded in any situation more by the friendship trigger than by logic, data, facts, and figures.

On a personal level, I have benefited handsomely with the friendship trigger. In one example, I met with the president and vice president of a training company interested in licensing the intellectual property rights to one of our programs.

I noticed the president limping. He had torn his knee cartilage playing racquetball, and required an operation. I had already had the operation he needed. We talked about knees for some time— shared interest! When asked, I learned that he started his own training company about the same time I did—shared interest, we're in similar time frames. I asked how he got his business start; same as mine. Through questions, I uncovered a good deal of common background and interests. We were building friendship and trust before even getting into the details. The licensing arrangement was quickly and easily finalized.

How can you benefit from the friendship trigger? How can you be liked, be a friend to an acquaintance, or someone you don't even know well?

We all prefer to deal with people we believe to be like us. Think about it—who would you be more likely to trust and be comfortable with? Would it be someone who has similar interests as you, who dresses somewhat the same, who shares similar backgrounds, ideals, and values, or someone with totally different background, values, views, and opinions? Someone with whom you have little in common? We are more comfortable and more responsive to those we perceive to be like us, and are cautious, adversely triggered by those we think are very different.

THE 7 TRIGGERS TO YES

"FITTING IN" FOR SUCCESS

What's the best way to activate your partner's internal trigger for friendship? Actually, it's pretty easy—easier than most realize.

The strongest element in the friendship equation is similarity: sameness. To be perceived as a friend, seek out and talk about common interests, whether business or personal, social, or geopolitical. These common interests can be literally anything—football, golf, theater, boating, fashion, raising kids, or building a business. We react more positively to those who share our dress style, our socioeconomic background, our values, and our opinions. The secret to presenting an aura of similarity is simply to learn enough about your partner to access those areas you can discuss and honestly be in concert with. This pre-work is absolutely essential to activate the friendship trigger. Successful persuasion is serious, demanding work.

Where do you start? If you are in another person's office or home, look around, clues will be abundant. Check her desk, items on the walls. Are there pictures of kids? Ask about them! Are there awards, plaques, pictures, anything that will add to your awareness? Any books or magazines? Ask questions about any of these items; then sit back and let them talk. A friend is a better listener than talker. And you don't learn anything when you're talking.

Suppose the person you hope to persuade is somewhat unknown to you. The wonderful news is that today, with the help of the Internet, you can learn almost anything about anyone. Give it a try—put anyone's name into a Google or Yahoo! search. There is a wealth of search engines that can provide you with almost any information you will ever want to know about your partner. If you are in a situation where prior research isn't practical, you can still learn about your partner's interests. How? Ask!

If they have kids, ask about them. If they are interested in sports, find out what they like. Ask and listen! Then find areas of mutual interest.

How might you establish the friendship trigger with someone very different from you and your background? What can you do to create warm friendly feelings with foreigners, business associates, or clients from other countries? With those whose cultures are very different from yours? There are many universal topics such as family, travel, business, sports, entertainment, and investments and these can serve as subjects for shared interests. In today's fast-shrinking world, it's important to be able to establish friendship with people of all cultures and backgrounds. The good news is that this can be easily accomplished.

ACTIVATING THE FRIENDSHIP TRIGGER

How do we put the friendship trigger to work? I needed an operation and wanted the best doctor in the field to perform it. The doctor I wanted was not taking new patients. He had the reputation of being a real curmudgeon—very difficult to talk to—and he had to get people in and out quickly. As chairman at a prestigious New York hospital's medical school and hospital, he was a very busy man. Other patients told me he was difficult to engage in conversation—make it business only, and be quick.

Employing every friendship trigger I could summon, I persuaded his appointment secretary to at least get me in for a consultation. In our first meeting, I asked the surgeon what he did when not working so hard. He gave me a rather surprised look and said he loved blue water sailboat racing. Now I'm not a sail enthusiast, but I am a boater, and we got onto the pleasures and challenges of boating. To my amazement he ushered me around his side of the desk, went to his computer, and pulled up his yacht club Web site.

His racing yacht was pictured on the site, along with all the yacht's racing credits.

In a follow-up meeting I applied the reciprocity trigger which is described later. I located a series of early 1900s issues of *Yachting Magazine,* which in those days were totally dedicated to sailing. I packaged them up and got them to the secretary to present the gift. He loved them! In each subsequent meeting the first question I asked was, "What's new with the yacht?" And each time I was regaled with racing stories, new Kevlar sail purchases, new state-of-the-art GPS electronics, etc.

The doctor had an extraordinarily well-documented success record for his work, and was intent on keeping his record intact. He kept score. He was therefore extremely selective as to whom he would operate on. My ability to activate his internal triggers helped me persuade him to operate on me. The world's top surgeon in the field did my operation, and with the help of a few triggers I'm alive today.

IS DRESS IMPORTANT?

How about dress? Is it important for the friendship trigger? Believe it! The secret is to dress similarly to the person you're trying to persuade. The more we dress like those we're working with, the better the perception of friendship. What happens when we dress wrong? I had an opportunity to make a training product presentation to a group of high-powered executives at a multi-billion-dollar company. Most of the execs were women. I was concerned because a large competitor, better positioned than my company, was also asked to make a presentation to the same group on the same day.

To my chagrin they were sending their top vice-president, a woman, to present to the women execs. This woman had cleverly scheduled to go last, the place I wanted to be. I knew I was facing a difficult battle.

The execs were in a very competitive, conservative, low-pay industry. To generate friendship and compatibility you must act as poor as they think they are. My competitor, a very attractive woman, entered the presentation room just as I was finishing. She was decked out in the most glamorous full-length mink coat I had ever seen. It was stunning! Her designer suit and jewelry were out of *Vogue*. She looked fabulous! And she was dead meat! Not a soul in this executive group could remotely identify with her. She didn't establish the friendship trigger. She was there to impress—she did! We were there to persuade—and we did! Against big odds, we persuaded principally because the competition violated the friendship trigger.

The simple lesson: make the friendship trigger work for you. Present an image your partner can positively identify with.

We have a great true story about a representative for a company trying to persuade several elements of a large manufacturing operation. Meeting at the executive level, he was "buttoned up"—suit, tie, the works. When he met with the foremen and supervisors he had his coat over his arm and tie loosened. When he met with the union workers, the tie was gone, the sleeves were rolled up. What was he doing? Probably unknown to him, he was practicing a huge element of the friendship trigger—he was mirroring his audience. With support from every element involved in the decision, decisions were made in his favor.

MIRRORING IS CRITICAL

Mirroring your partner is an important step in the friendship trigger. Knowing how the amygdala works, we now know how mirroring works. Mirroring simply means matching your partner's style, dress, and actions. If your partner is laid back with a laissez-faire approach to life, take it slowly! Don't come on like a hard-charging city slicker.

Conversely, if your partner is a high-powered, fast-paced guy, don't linger and dawdle. Get to the point and match his style. Actually mirroring his actions, sitting back and relaxing when he does, even mirroring frowns and smiles, activates the friendship trigger. This is not "monkey see monkey do," but simply a way to trigger the amygdala that "hey, I'm like you."

Researcher and pioneer in the field of sales psychology Dr. Donald Moine videotaped top persuaders making presentations. These super-performers were found to be mirroring the people they were trying to persuade. But here's the interesting, unexpected discovery. In slow-motion replay, it was noted that these top pros were actually breathing in and out in sync with the other person! They were subconsciously totally mirroring the client. To successfully persuade, you don't have to breathe in and out with your partner. You must, however, create feelings of similarity that will trigger the amygdala in your favor.

There are very specific questions that work magic to activate your partner's friendship trigger. The sidebar "Trigger Elements" provides some thoughts you might build into your presentation framework.

Establishing common ground, showing interest in and support for the other person, is what friendship is all about. Whether you know your partner well, not so well, or not at all, the trigger elements will help you establish or reaffirm the common bonds of friendship and trust. Friends are better listeners than talkers. Ask, listen, and you'll quickly and easily activate the trigger of friendship.

TRIGGER ELEMENTS

To establish or renew friendship, ask about any of the following—then listen attentively!

Leisure time—how do you spend it?

"What do you like to do when you're not working so hard?" This question is one of the easiest ways to get someone talking about his interests and passions. Anyone who is interested in what he is interested in is a friend.

Kids

If they have them, they love to talk about them. You're a friend for asking—and listening.

Background

"Where are you from originally?" "What brought you here?" Simple questions to open a dialogue that can go on and on.

Business

"How did you get started in this business?" "How did you become so good at your work?" Any questions related to business background will delight your partner. You'll often find parallels with your own, leading to friendly discussions.

Education

"Where did you go to school?" "What did you major in?" These are great questions to open an entire category about education and skills. People love to talk about their education and how they got to be so smart.

Sports

If they're into it, go for it! Fans enjoy talking about their teams and heroes. Ask the question about the latest game and let them roll! And when you can, agree with them.

Travel

Those who travel for business or pleasure love to talk about their special places. They either love or hate the traveling—share the enthusiasm, or commiserate with the downsides. Either way you're being friendly.

TV shows

Playing couch potato is a popular pastime. Ask what they like, find common interests, and seek out agreement with your partner's tastes.

Movies

If you learn she has seen the latest blockbuster, ask her views—she won't be shy! Be a good listener and mention perceptions you agree with.

Spouse or relationships

This one is tricky, but often good if there are situations similar to yours. If that is the case, it's easy to establish common ground.

Friends

Friends of friends are friends. Ask, find common connections. Mutual acquaintances are great topics for friendly discussions.

Music

If you have interests here and find common ground, explore it.

Pets

Some think more about their pets than their kids. Some have unusual pets. Many will talk endlessly about the pets they love.

Local events

If they are involved in community, theater, whatever, get them talking about events past, present, and future. They'll appreciate your interest.

Associations and clubs

Almost everyone is involved in groups of some sort. Learn what your partner joins and why. Then agree where you can that these are great groups to be involved with. Church, charity affiliations are things those involved in love to talk about.

Give thanks or appreciation

A key human motivator is appreciation from others. Find something you can show thanks and appreciation for and do it. Express appreciation for the time spent together. Appreciation is a foundation of friendship.

Give approval or commendation

Friends approve and praise friends. Approval is a form of liking, and always appreciated. Show approval, appreciation for any action or deed, small or large.

Give positive, not negative, input

Positive reinforcement creates positive action and feeling. Negative input, even if "helpful," creates the reverse. Be careful how you position negative comments. Better yet, avoid them.

Accomplishments

It's easy to learn what your partner has accomplished—just ask around. If you don't know, ask her! You'll be a friend for talking—and listening—about the accomplishments.

Skills and abilities

Everyone has special skills, and is proud of them! Learn these skills, share in one's pride, and you'll be a friend.

Intelligence

"How did you get that done so well?" "That was really a clever approach." We all think we're pretty smart—a friend will reinforce the image!

Ability to work with others

"It seems you're pretty good with people to get so much done through others." We all pride our people skills, and love those who recognize this skill.

Avoid controversial issues

Politics, religion, sex, and other controversial issues are generally off-limits since the potential downsides are greater than the upside. Unless you're 100 percent certain that you are in full agreement (seldom happens) with your partner on one of these issues, stay away! These can be quicksand. If he brings up one of these issues, use another question to move on to a more promising subject.

Praise

Praise is a universal doorway to friendship. We love those who praise us; they are friends. Find something to praise. Be sincere. Do it.

Mirroring

All of these help you establish mirroring. In short, mirroring is simply acting like the other person. Being interested in what they are interested in, sharing ideas and views, dressing in similar fashion. And yes, mirroring their actions, pace, and intonation. The more we appear like the partner and the closer we are to how they perceive themselves, the more friendly we appear.

Do your homework. Learn as much about your partner as possible. Ask questions to learn interests you might relate to. Be friendly and honest and you'll be trusted.

BUILD YOUR FOUNDATION ON FRIENDSHIP

Preparing for the friendship trigger is work—critical, maybe even hard, yet beneficial work. Before your meeting, check the items previously listed. Then plan and list all the things you can do and say to create a feeling of similarity, of shared interests. When you've established friendship, you can tackle the persuasion issues with a goal of shared success. Employ the friendship trigger well and you'll build a strong foundation for the rest of your persuasive communication.

REVIEW AND REFERENCE

- Persuading others is easy when people like you, when they consider you a friend. Friendship generates trust, and trust activates a strong internal trigger.
- Liking is a prerequisite for most other triggers to be effective. We all prefer to deal with people we believe to be like us.
- The best way to activate your partner's internal trigger for friendship is through similarity. Seek out and talk about common interests. Learn enough about your partner to access those areas you can discuss and honestly be in concert with.
- Do your homework. Learn as much about your partner as possible. Ask questions to learn about interests you might relate to. A friend is a better listener than talker.
- By asking others, by checking Internet search engines like Google or Yahoo!, you can find out almost anything about anyone.
- Mirroring your partner is an important step in the friendship trigger. Match your partner's style of dress and actions.
- Always present an image your partner can positively identify with.
- Before your meeting, plan and list all the things you can do and say to create a feeling of similarity, through shared interests. Then tackle the issues at hand with a goal of shared success.
- For your CPO, current persuasion opportunity, we have an interactive form to help determine the most persuasive elements for the friendship trigger. Go to www.seventriggers.com where you can select the applicable elements, make notes, and print them out.

Chapter 9

Authority Trigger

W hen your partner believes you know what you're talking about, when you're perceived as an authority on your subject, you're well on your way to easy, successful persuasion. We respond with unthinking, automatic compliance to those we believe have authority, credibility, and power. Establish your authority, credibility, and expertise and your partner's amygdala quickly and automatically makes a positive decision. The *authority trigger* is so strong that, when perceived, the amygdala doesn't even send information to the prefrontal cortex for further cognitive evaluation. You're home free.

Remember Caesar Augustus with his *Vini Vidi Vici* opening: "I came, I saw, I conquered"?

After his defeat of King Pharnaces, his victory over Pompei, and his installation of Cleopatra as queen of Egypt, he established credibility as a warrior and administrator. With a simple three-word statement, Caesar Augustus demonstrated his authority and credibility in a powerful manner. No analysis was required. The amygdala was triggered and his followers were quickly on board.

REDUCE RISK

Decisions involve risk. And as part of the limbic system, the amygdala is very sensitive to risk. Keep in mind the fight-or-flight, immediate decision. When you are perceived as an authority, your partner perceives less risk, feels more assurance and trust in the decision you help him make. Sincerity, honesty, competency, enthusiasm, and accuracy reduce risk for your partner.

AUTHORITY TRIGGERS COMPLIANCE

Aristotle established ethos as one of the major elements in persuasion. In his book *Rhetoric,* Aristotle wrote, "Character is, almost, so to speak, the controlling factor in persuasion." Authority is the power to persuade, to influence, to sell an idea based on your knowledge, expertise, and experience. Let your character be perceived as that of a knowledgeable authority.

Why is this important? Because we give automatic, unthinking compliance to authority. We automatically accept what the lawyer says on legal issues, what the CPA tells us on finance or tax issues, what the doctor or nurse says on medical issues. No evaluative thinking is required. We perceive that they've done the difficult work for us.

When someone we accept as an authority suggests something, we abandon the hard work required to do our own research. We gladly take the easy, safe, automatic, and comfortable road to persuasion and compliance. We let the "expert" do the pick and shovel work. We trust the authority, and based on that trust we coast to agreement. Compliance is easy and convenient.

Even before we knew how the amygdala and the cerebral cortex interact, we were aware that authority was an important element in persuasion. The Greeks established the concept. Later, Sigmund Freud postulated that "source credibility" is an innate human need for decision making. To fill this source credibility need to make the right decision, we often seek out someone we view as an expert, at least someone better qualified than ourselves. Whether it's a friend, co-worker, boss, parent, or professional we want to feel comfortable that we are making the right decision. When we get input from an authority, our need for source credibility is fulfilled. This allows us to make the right decisions automatically, quickly, and without the pain of arduous cognitive evaluation.

With the results of in vivo brain imaging, we can see how the brain responds to credible information. We can watch the amygdala make immediate judgments when it perceives authoritative stimuli. Because the amygdala is so risk sensitive, we understand why credibility is so critical to persuasion, and we know how to apply authority to gain easy, quick compliance. Properly presented, the authority trigger motivates automatic quick compliance from the amygdala. The amygdala preempts time-consuming evaluative thinking.

CREDIBILITY DOES THE CONVINCING

As one example, we accept with unthinking automatic compliance what the doctor says. When the doctor gives you a prescription, do you evaluate the chemical compounds in the pill, check the FDA reams of data for approvals, or do you go to the pharmacy and get the prescription filled? When the CPA gives you a definitive answer on a tax issue, do you head for the library or the IRS Web site and personally research the incomprehensible tax code? Or do you comply with your CPA?

Do we respond intellectually, with lots of cognitive evaluation, or do we respond automatically to those we perceive to be in a position of authority? Years ago our company was asked to produce a training program for the Aetna Insurance Group. It would not have been cost-effective to produce the program only for Aetna, and I didn't think the program they requested would sell to others. Intellectually, logically, I was very reluctant to invest company assets in the project.

The head of the Aetna Institute, their prestigious training facility, was Ed Higgeson. Ed requested a personal meeting, and reminded me that the Aetna Institute had recently been awarded the American Society for Training and Development's designation as the top training company in America. That's credibility. Ed had already established his personal credibility, his authority. He wore his Phi Beta Kappa key and his prestigious insurance professional CPCU designation on his tie chain. More authority. Without saying a word, Ed convinced me that he was smart and knowledgeable about insurance training issues. Against my rational, cognitive better judgment, my amygdala, my internal authority trigger persuaded me to invest time, personnel resources, and a good deal of money to produce the training Ed requested. To my amazement the resultant program became our best, most profitable seller.

It is a common belief that the more critical the issue, the more we will use cognitive thinking rather than emotional triggers to evaluate a situation. Not necessarily. When Hewlett-Packard was in a proxy fight to take over Compaq Computer, billions of dollars were at risk for those with large holdings in either of the two companies. The stakes were huge, literally mind-boggling. Shareholder polling indicated the odds were against approval of the acquisition.

Carli Fiorina, then Hewlett-Packard CEO, was asked in an interview with Bloomberg Radio's Fred Fishkin how people could evaluate and decide on the incredibly complex issues investors faced in voting their shares. Fiorina said, "If you don't have the time or the experience to evaluate the merits I suggest you look at the ISS decision." ISS, the highly regarded Institutional Shareholder Services company, had already recommended the merger to its institutional stockholder subscribers. Accepting the authority of the ISS, and without a lot of cognitive evaluation, the acquisition was approved by shareholders.

The authority trigger is so incredibly powerful, it often transcends areas of specific knowledge and expertise. We look so favorably on the legal information lawyers provide that we regularly seek their opinion on business issues. This is usually a mistake. When they advise on issues outside the realm of law, lawyers often motivate delays and bad business decisions.

Here's a personal example. We were nearing finalization of a major training and consulting contract with a multinational telecommunications company, needing only final law review of a 37-page contract. All the business decisions had been finalized with company executives. We met with their law department, got everything agreed to with one exception, a "small change," as the lawyers called it, regarding copyright ownership of the final product. Management had agreed that if we reduced our price to produce the program, we would own the copyright. Because the company was paying for the development of the program, the lawyers asserted, their company must own the copyright. Had I not realized the lawyers were well outside their expertise and authority area, we might not have ever been able to sell the program to anyone else. This issue had been thoroughly explored and agreed to by management. We were at an impasse.

I simply asked, "Are you the law department?" They puffed out their chests and said they were indeed Mega Company's law department. I suggested the issue at question was a business issue, not a law issue, and that the lawyers were outside their realm. I recommended rather strongly that they stick to legal issues. They finally agreed, after almost costing their company the opportunity to have a program they wanted and badly needed. The lesson: know the authority areas you are dealing with. Don't be persuaded by issues outside the persuader's area of expertise. And, in your persuasion attempts, do your best to establish your own authority and expertise in the specific area you are dealing with.

SOURCE CREDIBILITY PERSUADES

This example points to a critical aspect of how we perceive expertise and authority. Hundreds of scientific studies have been conducted to determine the validity of source credibility. Several studies have evaluated responses to similar statements attributed to various sources. The results never vary. The more credible the perception of the source, the more credible the source's statement appears. For example, which of the following quotes would you be more likely to believe?

> "Computer science is in its infancy. In the near future we will be running our households from computers the size of today's cell phones."—Jay Leno

> "Computer science is in its infancy. In the near future we will be running our households from computers the size of today's cell phones."—Bill Gates

Here's a real-world example of perceived source authority. In a Yale University study, two groups of volunteers each heard the same factual argument in favor of selling antihistamines without prescription. One group was told the source for the proposal was a popular pictorial magazine. The other group was given a fictional source called *The New England Journal of Biology and Medicine*.

Which source was more persuasive? Right! *The New England Journal of Biology and Medicine*. Why? It sounds more authoritative. The perception of authority influenced the vote.

BE THE EXPERT—ESTABLISH CREDIBILITY

Now that we've established that the strength of authority is a persuader, how do you apply and benefit from this powerful internal trigger?

The short answer is easy. Be the expert. Do your homework. Know your stuff. Establish your credibility and authority. Ethos, authority, is not an absolute. It is the interpretation, the perception others have regarding you. Your task is to employ every means available to establish this all-important perception.

If you already have the expertise and information required to create the right perception, great! If you do not have it, get it! Do the research. Know your products, services, your company, and all relevant material inside and out. Pick the brains of other experts. Hire a consultant. Find a professor at a local college. Search the net. Get help from anyone with more knowledge than you. Do all you can to establish your credibility. Let your partner know that you are fully informed about your topic, and that you can be trusted to give expert information.

When is the best time to share your authority, your expertise with your partner? Early and often! The sooner you establish your credibility, the easier your persuasion will be. When I have a speaking, consulting, or training engagement, I let people know right up front that I have significant knowledge, experience, and expertise in persuasion, decision management, or whatever we're working on. This experience and expertise help to tailor your comments to each situation.

Tailoring is important, because everyone thinks their situation is different. We do a fair amount of work within the property and casualty insurance industry, and they perceive themselves to be very different from any other business. They want to deal with people who really understand their business. If I'm working with an insurance group, I tell them up front that I served as an executive with a major property and casualty insurance company. I share with them the fact that I was elected to the presidency of the Insurance Managers Association, and that I received the Insurance Man of the Year Award from that association. I quickly point out that I am in no way bragging, just letting them know that I understand their business. Been there, done that. I then do not have to justify my comments, since I've set the stage, delineated my experience and expertise. I've established my credibility, my authority. It works!

If we're dealing with a communications or high-tech company, I share with them that we partnered with the world's largest communications company to create programs specific to their various entities. I will show some of the work we produced for that company. If it's banking, I tell them about the large consulting contract we had with a top player in the Fortune 500, and note how we helped the company increase growth and profit. The comments are all accurate, all true, yet tailored to the authority sought in each situation. You get the idea. Set your authority to honestly and realistically show the partner how much experience and expertise you have in the specific area under discussion.

Be precise and specific in your communications. Instead of stating, "This will help reduce cost," say, "We have documented stats to show this approach will cut payroll costs by 6.8 percent." We use very specific data to establish credibility for our training programs. We show a letter from a multi-billion-dollar company that documents in writing an 11.4 percent revenue growth from those who were trained in our program as compared to those trained in-house. That's credibility! That's the kind of authority that triggers compliance.

We show another letter on a client letterhead verifying the company's annual savings of $3.8 million that the company attributes to the reduced cost of department turnover after our training. Compare that to, "We'll save you a lot of money." By using specific data rather than banal generalities, we become a more credible authority. By being specific you are perceived as an expert—someone who does the homework. Your partner will know you did the heavy exertion so that he doesn't have to. Put simply, that's the impression you must achieve—that you've done the work and you're the one your partner can rely upon. You build trust and confidence. Knowledge backed up with proof is a strong persuader.

Is dress important for establishing authority? Bet on it! Remember the poor dress choice—the mink coat in the *friendship* trigger section? If you want to be perceived as "one of us," one of the gang, someone we can relate to and have confidence in, dress the part. I had a good example of dress and authority in staid old Boston. I was given the opportunity to make a presentation to eight executives of a stuffy Boston company, a company I did not know very well.

Luckily, one of the VPs called the day before I left and said, "Be sure to wear a dark blue suit and a white button-down shirt." When we sat down in their penthouse board room overlooking Boston Harbor, I noted nine blue suits, and nine button-down shirts. Boring? You bet, but I was as boring as the rest. I can only guess they viewed blue suits and white button-down shirts as symbols of authority. That was 12 years ago and we're still doing business with the company.

Dress, carriage, and nonverbal clues are components of authority. An IT techie can get away with less formal dress. Leaders and managers cannot. Create the right impression. And don't overdo it—no mink coat! Many facets of authority operate with considerable subtlety—take advantage of all of them.

One important caveat regarding your knowledge and expertise: do not fool yourself into believing you are more of an expert than you are. Harvard University, through the Harvard Business School, researched a vast array of management talent and ability. Their findings are revealing. In his article for the *Harvard Business Review* called "The Necessary Art of Persuasion," Jay Conger states, "Our research strongly suggests that most managers overestimate their credibility—considerably!"

The sad result of this overestimation is that everyone but you will know about it. When you think you know it all and wing it, you will never generate the influence you would with true expertise. The phonies get found out fast. Do your homework. Be credible. Be a true authority.

TRIGGER ELEMENTS

Consider these thoughts as you plan your conversation with your persuasion partner.

Establishing authority is easy, but not automatically perceived—she probably doesn't know as much about you as you think. To be effective in creating the best perceptions, you have to set the stage. Let your partner know you are not bragging—you just want to share important information. Here is a sample of the elements of authority that will activate your partner's authority trigger.

Dress and bearing

Look and act the role of the authority you are. Perception is reality—create the best possible perception for your image. First impressions count, yes, but recurring encounters are critical too—make each a good one.

Accomplishments

Share information about any awards, commendations, achievements, promotions, success stories on topics relevant to your subject. The more he knows of your past success, the more you will be perceived as an authority.

Research

It's critical to let your partner know you have done the hard work so that he doesn't have to. Let him know about your relevant research. Tell him about the books you read, the online searches, the databases examined, the experts you contacted.

Papers, articles, and books

If you've written anything relevant to your subject, show it! People tend to believe the written word. Authors are perceived as authorities on their subject.

Endorsements

Obtain, then share positive comments from anyone who has worked with you or agrees with your premise. It's easy to get endorsements—just ask! Positive input about you is stronger when it comes from others.

Success documentation

Show any items that back up your premise. The better you document your authority, the better perceptions you generate.

Speeches and presentations

If you've made them, tell your partner. Provide copies if available. They demonstrate knowledge, expertise.

Established credibility

If others have endorsed, written about, or achieved success from relevant ideas, share the information. This actuates several triggers.

Education

Share the background for your knowledge and expertise. If education at a specific department of a specific school is relevant, shout it. Note how doctors, lawyers, and other professionals prominently display these icons of authority.

Degrees

Let your partner know about any academic or professional degrees relevant to your topic. Mention any courses relevant to the subject. Background knowledge is important to perceptions.

Awards

If any awards or commendations are applicable, talk about them. Sometimes awards, if not directly applicable, are transferable, and it can't hurt to share any award information.

Training

Any training specific to your subject is important to establishing credibility and expertise. Let them know you're well qualified.

Titles

Titles convey power, influence. If you have them, use them. If you've had them in the past, refer to them. Same if you're expecting a new one. Virtually everyone has a title conveying credibility in her area. Titles work.

Affiliations

Memberships in organizations and professional associations are always documented to show expertise and authority. If memberships are relevant, use them.

Professional designations

Every industry has its professional designations. We see those letters and acronyms on many business cards. If you have them, show them. If you don't have them, think about getting them!

Experience

When your partner knows you have "been there, done that," you are perceived as an authority. Real-world experience trumps almost anything else to establish authority. Catalogue your key, most relevant experiences and share them.

Achievements

Experience is important—documented achievement is better. Cite any relevant achievements—the more the better.

Promotions

Promotions are an indication of expertise and they generate perceptions of authority. Without bragging, factually let her know about promotions, including the reasons.

Specialized knowledge or expertise

Research, education, and experience lead to specialized knowledge. If that knowledge is relevant, share what you know and how you know it.

Relationships with authority figures

Who have you worked with, met with, researched, learned from to enhance your own knowledge? If these relationships exist, use them! Piggybacking on another's expertise is a smart and realistic way to enhance your own.

Background qualifications

Much of the above can be assembled and then employed to create the background for your expertise, your authority. While difficult to synthesize into a *"Vini Vidi Vici"* capsule, do your best to distill the information, then show how your background documents your expertise.

AUTHORITY RULES

Researchers have found that ethos, authority, is a major controlling factor in our lives, our business, and in our politics.

Zig Ziglar, author of *See You at the Top,* heads a training company that conducted a study on persuasion and perceptions. The tabulated results indicated that 65 percent of persuasion situations were headed in the right, or wrong, direction based solely on the perceptions the other person had of the persuader. Is this so surprising when we know how juries react to the perception of the lawyer and the opening statements?

Connecticut Superior Court Judge Douglas Levine trains lawyers in persuasion skills. In his excellent book *Cardinal Rules of Advocacy,* he makes an analogy between real estate and persuasion. "Where the key to real estate value is location, location, location, the key to persuasion is credibility, credibility, credibility." Levine writes, "If you take nothing else from this book, let it be this. The advocate's [persuader's] credibility is without question his most precious asset. I liken it to oxygen in a scuba diver's tank."

By creating the perception of authority and expertise, ethos can be one of your most precious persuasion assets. Ethos is the persuader's oxygen—make it your persuasion lifeline. Establish your ethos, and your partner's amygdala will never have to send your information to the cerebral cortex for painful, lengthy cognitive evaluation. You'll earn quick, virtually automatic compliance.

REVIEW AND REFERENCE

- We respond with unthinking automatic compliance to those we believe have authority, credibility, and power. Establish your authority, credibility, and expertise and your partner's amygdala quickly and automatically makes a positive decision.
- We give unthinking automatic compliance to authority because we believe they have done the difficult work for us. We do what the authority suggests because it's easy and convenient.
- Source credibility is an innate need for human decision making. To fill the source credibility needed to make the right decision, we often seek an expert. This allows us to make the right decisions, automatically, quickly, and without the pain of cognitive evaluation.
- Do your best to establish your own authority and expertise in the specific areas you are dealing with. Be the expert, do your homework. Let your partner know that you are fully informed about your topic and that you can be trusted to give expert information.
- Dress, carriage, and nonverbal clues are also components of authority. Create the right impression and your partner will perceive less risk, feel more assurance, and trust in the decision you help him make.

- Beware of self-deception, believing you know more than you do. When you think you know it all and wing it, you will never generate the influence you would with true expertise.
- For your CPO, current persuasion opportunity, we have an interactive form to help determine the most persuasive elements for the authority trigger. Go to www.seventriggers.com where you can select the applicable elements, make notes, and print them out.

Chapter 10

Consistency Trigger

ere's a persuasion truism to log into the memory bank. We are slaves to *consistency* and conformity.

Our internal guidance system compels us to be consistent with the way we see ourselves and the way we see our admired peers. From birth we create an internal databank of beliefs and past performance. We use these as an easy, safe, comfortable, nonthinking guide to make current decisions and to generate action. Voters tend to vote with the party. Thrifty people don't go for all the bells and whistles. Savers save; spenders spend. Liberals act liberal; conservatives act conservatively. Risk takers are adventurous; risk avoiders are cautious.

Consistency and conformity are primal instincts governed by the amygdala. Watch a flock of birds or a school of fish turn in a split second and follow the leader—we're no different. We laugh when others laugh, cry when others cry, glance up at the sky as others do. We are required to be consistent with what's in our database and to conform to what our peers do.

NAVIGATING WITH EMOTIONAL MEMORY

The neuroscientists who contributed to *The Secret Life of the Brain* series clearly describe how consistency works: "All the things you go through in life in terms of decisions are inevitably accompanied by some kind of emotion; each decision has some similarity to a decision of the past. When you are in a position to decide once again, you'll call up an emotional memory that leads you in one direction or another."

As noted by neuroscientist Dr. Antonio Damasio, "So what you have is literally a navigational aid; something that gets you to the right decision. If that is broken down, you'd be at the mercy of facts and logic and that's just not good enough."

The research findings are clear. Decisions are emotion-based. Facts and logic simply cannot influence our decisions the way emotions do.

You can give someone who believes very strongly in an issue all of the logical, rational reasons why he should change those beliefs but you'd be wasting two people's time. How many people would change their beliefs about the Christmas holiday if informed that the birth of Christ actually occurred in March? What would change if they were informed that Christmas—and its timing—was actually a continuation of older pagan tradition worshiping the winter solstice?

Roman Catholic writer Mario Righetti writes in *The Manual of Liturgical History* that "to facilitate the acceptance of the faith by the pagan masses, the Church of Rome found it convenient to institute the 25th of December as the feast of the birth of Christ." This was initiated, Righetti explained, "to divert them from the pagan feast, celebrated on the same day in honor of the 'Invincible Sun' Mithras, the conqueror of darkness." Christmas should be celebrated in March, but historical fact has little or no impact on centuries of belief, celebration, and tradition. Religious, racial, ethnic, political, and similar perceptions are oblivious to logic, facts, and figures. Attempting to alter views in these arenas is a study in futility. Yet the key to persuasion is to recognize that virtually everything we perceive is held as an indelible memory. Work with your partner's amygdala, not against it.

Since beliefs, values, feelings, and perceptions have little to do with fact and logic, you succeed better by working in concert with your partner's perceptions. For each of us reality is whatever we perceive it to be.

Thus as foreign as it may be from your own, your partner's perception is his reality. Learn his reality and work with it.

ACTIVATE INTERNAL GUIDANCE

Consistency is acting in consonance with one's past experience, values, feelings, and perceptions. Being consistent with these experiences makes us comfortable. It makes us confident that we are making the right decision. And since the amygdala has saved all those prior experiences for us, being consistent acts as a precise navigation system to help us determine the best of several choices. The amygdala helps us make these choices, consistent with our concept of self. When we make decisions and generate actions inconsistent with our self-image, we are nervous and uncomfortable and seek ways to solve the inconsistency.

We persuade by making people comfortable. Consistency is the internal trigger that motivates us to be and to act the same as those we positively relate to. We each have "reference groups" we look to for consistency and we work hard to be consistent with these groups; to conform to those sharing our views. The way school kids dress is an example of consistency through conformity. Within peer groups, the most important thing is to look the same: wear the same hairstyles, the same sneakers. Conversely, ignore this need for consistency and you generate internal dissonance. Worse yet, stray from peer group consistency and you risk social sanction.

As Mark Twain said in "Corn-Pone Opinions," "It is in our nature to conform, it is a force which not many of us can resist." For the first time, we now know how this internal trigger works and can apply it for the benefit of all concerned. Our internal guidance system requires us to be consistent with two categories of expectations—our own, and those of our admired peers.

HIT AND MISS WON'T DO IT

Historically we didn't know how or why this trigger worked, yet marketers have been applying consistency on a hit-or-miss basis for years. Have you ever entered a contest where you were asked to write why you like a product? Cereal, dessert, and food companies benefited handsomely from these "contests."

When you completed the statement, you were creating a file in your mental databank that requires you to be consistent the next time you shop for that product. When you looked at the competing brands on the shelf, the amygdala pointed you to the right product. This is in large part what brand identity is all about. No cognitive thought required. We automatically pick up the right product and toss it into the basket.

Here's another application of consistency. Before making a purchase you might vacillate about the decision. Yet after the decision is made, you love the choice. You are being consistent with your selection, your prior action. We see this every day in our training business. After a pilot program, the client always has some doubts, but then after they purchase the program they virtually always become ardent supporters and provide great references. They will be consistent with the information that created the decision to purchase.

Perhaps the best (or worst, in my view) example of the application of consistency is in the entertainment field. As with other triggers, we learned by trial and error that this trigger works, but until recently we were not sure how or why. Yet almost 200 years ago theater owners in France realized that as we see others reacting to a performance, we act like lemmings. Thus when a small group of theatergoers cheered, the rest cheered too. When a small group booed or hissed, the rest usually followed. If a few gave a standing ovation, the rest rose in applause; and if the small group laughed loudly and boisterously . . . well, you get the idea.

As early as the 1820s, businesses were formed in France to sell their services to theaters. Employees of these companies were hired by the opera and theater owners to laugh, applaud, stand, and cheer at very specific points in the show. With no thought or logic, it worked; so much so that these planted shills became big business.

And they still are! As kids, my mother often took us to see "live, spontaneous" radio shows in New York City. Even as a kid I was amazed that the live audience was totally controlled by on-stage employees who raised large printed signs telling the audience when to laugh, cheer, and applaud. In order to gain compliance from the radio listening audience, the "live" audience was totally controlled.

LAUGH TRACK CONSISTENCY

And of course today we have a daily reminder of the consistency trigger at its most ubiquitous application. We are absolute suckers for this consistency trigger—yes, the TV laugh track! Without the laugh track, sitcoms would be nonexistent. Most shows are appallingly poor, yet helped along by the laugh track, they survive. Through the consistency trigger, they get us to laugh or at least chuckle as the nonaudience canned track "laughs" at the poor material.

Even the few quality shows would not make it without the laugh track. Jerry Seinfeld fought studio heads in a "knock-down drag-out" battle in his quest to eliminate the laugh track from his far-above-average sitcom. He thought his show was good enough to succeed without it. The studio finally convinced Seinfeld his show would fold without it. The laugh track stayed. It produces mindless automatic, easy conformity. The canned phantoms laugh, and we laugh. The show is funny; we'll watch it next time. The advertisers stay.

The consistency trigger works with incredible reliability. We easily demonstrate this trigger during our persuasion training. At the beginning of the workshop we tell one attendee that we will congratulate her for some imaginary achievement, say a minor promotion. We ask two or three others to applaud when this is announced. We make the announcement and watch as everyone in the room applauds. But applauds for what? They do not even know her. They have no idea what they were applauding for. All they know is that the consistency trigger, conformity, kicked in. Two other trainees applauded, so they did too.

Consistency appears to be one of those triggers fully developed in the amygdala at birth. I recently attended an outdoor concert by one of the U.S. Navy's bands—the Commodores. A toddler, just over one year old, still in diapers, was walking with her dad with her back to the band. As a piece finished, we were applauding. To my amazement, this toddler shook off her father's hand and began clapping herself. She certainly didn't know why. She couldn't even see the band, yet the consistency trigger kicked in! She had to be consistent—and so do we! Whenever there is uncertainty in our information or decision process, we look to what's being done by others we respect and then conform to that.

Interestingly, there's almost always some uncertainty when we have to decide. We tend to be consistent with even those we don't know, but perceive to be like us. The extraordinary success of Zagat's restaurant guides is a prime example. Zagat's guides are built on nothing more than ordinary people's evaluations of the restaurants they visit. Diners send in their ratings, Zagat's compiles them, sells them to us, and we comply—we go to the restaurants others rate highly.

Applying the internal consistency trigger is very easy. The hard part is to learn what your partner will be consistent with. In a phone conversation with a company president, I asked what had made him so successful. One of the answers he gave me was that he made quick decisions, then acted on them. At the end of a face-to-face presentation with this executive, there were still many licensing issues to be resolved. Since I'd traveled 2,000 miles for the meeting, I didn't want to string out the process and return for another meeting. I reminded the president that he had mentioned that one of his strengths was making quick decisions. He agreed. I then asked, "Will your decision on this product follow your quick decision record?" He looked at me for a few seconds, smiled, and offered a "deal" handshake. He was required to be consistent with his self-image as a quick decision maker. I learned what he would be consistent with; he executed, and we both made money on the deal.

Ever hear of the adage, "You get what you pay for?" We often believe higher price is consistent with higher quality. When Bob Miller was president of the Charles of the Ritz cosmetics and fragrance company, he worked with Yves St. Laurent to create a new perfume called "Opium."

Yves St. Laurent had the reputation of being the world's top fashion designer. Opium had to be perceived as having the same high quality as other YSL products. It had to be consistent with the YSL image and the YSL high-priced product line. St. Laurent's dresses sold for thousands of dollars, and Miller and St. Laurent wanted to generate the same image for the new perfume.

To enhance the perception of quality and value being equal to other YSL products, Miller priced Opium at the highest level— around $150 per ounce. As more and more women "discovered" Opium, more and more wanted to conform to the growing trend. Opium became the world's best-selling perfume, garnering more than 8 percent of the world market.

The interesting thing is that to manufacture the perfume in the Opium bottle cost virtually the same as most other brands. The cost/quality consistency, the YSL image, the consistency of "you get what you pay for" trigger paid off! Although there was no more inherent quality or value in Opium, the price, along with the high-end promotion, the desire to conform with the YSL image, made Opium fly off the shelves. The consistency trigger, equating price and image with value, made the brand. No thinking required. It's got to be good, buy it! They did.

One of the best examples of the consistency trigger at work is cigarette branding. Generations ago, a new cigarette brand was introduced. For years, the brand languished among many others and finally became invisible, scoring dead last in sales. To give the brand one last shot, the marketers decided to position it not for what it actually was but for what it could represent. The marketers created a personality that people would wish to identify with, be consistent with—the idea of rugged independence, virility, strength, clean open spaces. Well, sure, you've already figured it out: the Marlboro Man. Desired consistency with that representation took Marlboro from dead last to the world's top seller by 300 percent over the second place brand.

MEET THE CRITERIA, WIN THE DAY!

So here's the productive work you must do to help your partner benefit from her internal consistency trigger. Find out how your partner has acted in the past on issues such as those being discussed. Learn what she values, believes in, takes pride in; then frame your proposal to meet these criteria.

Facts and logic simply won't impact or change the long-established database that the amygdala has created. Do your homework. Research how your partner acted in situations similar to what you're proposing. Ask his friends, family, business associates for past performance data. Find out how he thinks and acts. Once you have the requisite information, frame your request so that his positive decision will be consistent with past actions.

TRIGGER ELEMENTS

The following will help you frame your persuasive communication.

The secret to activating your partner's consistency trigger is to learn what she will be consistent with. Here are things you'll want to learn about your partner.

Automatic or analytic mode

Decision and action modes seldom change. Consistency is virtually guaranteed. Learn which mode your partner employs, and frame your presentation accordingly. Remember that most people all of the time and all people most of the time are in the automatic mode.

Spending habits

Big spender or cheapskate? Keep up with the Joneses or pinch pennies? Bargain hunter or nothing but the best? Spending habits strongly influence many decisions. They are easy to learn and easy to match to your proposal.

Affiliations with clubs or associations

Is he a joiner? Knowledge about his affiliations will tell you precisely what he will be consistent with. Your homework on both your partner and each association pays off.

Social status

We strive for consistency with our status perceptions. Learn status of business, economic, and social peers and you'll know how to frame your comments.

Risk tolerance versus risk aversion

This is important and easy to learn. Seek out or ask for information on past decisions, actions, plans. Then show how your proposal provides fun, challenge, and high rewards for the attendant risk, or frame the idea differently to show how your idea can reduce risk.

Peer group values

Who are her peers? What are their values? She is likely to have many of the same values her peer group shares. Learn her friends, her work peers, her associates, and you'll learn values she'll be consistent with.

Political—conservative or liberal

Careful here—you don't want to discuss politics, yet you want to know what he'll be consistent with. Some wear their leanings on their sleeve—others will give you hints on their thinking. Learn what you can, because these issues are usually cast in stone, almost always triggering consistency.

Habits

We are slaves to our habits. We'll be consistent with our ingrained approaches. Seek out patterns and position your material to show consistency with prior actions.

Religious leanings

Careful here too, yet realize that the more you know about religious beliefs, the easier it will be to position your appeal wisely. We are consistent with our beliefs, so frame your idea to be consistent with her beliefs.

Self-perceptions

"How would you see yourself in this role?" "How might you feel about your part in making this change become reality?" Asking the right questions will inform you on self-perceptions. We'll always conform to how we see ourselves. Ask, listen, proceed accordingly.

Pride

What does your partner take pride in? Family, business success, personal growth, accomplishment? Ask and it will be answered. Pride is a huge motivator, a powerful internal trigger. "Think how proud you will be when this is done the way you can do it!"

Values

Honesty, integrity, hard work, giving back, fairness—the list of values is infinite. Ask around, ask your partner about specifics. He'll be consistent with the values you uncover.

Education

Bachelor of Arts or Bachelor of Science? Analytical or automatic courses? Learn the education details and you'll know more about what she'll be consistent with.

Prior decisions

Critical information. The more you know how past decisions were made with similar issues, the better you know what he will conform to for future decisions.

Prior actions

Learn all you can about how your partner acted in similar prior situations. As with decisions, she will be consistent with those prior situations.

Reference groups and peers

Check to see who she hangs out with at work and socially. Chances are good that you'll acquire relevant information about whom and what she'll be consistent with and conform to. Like kids in school, we conform to the values of perceived peers.

Papers, articles, and books

Any writings you can gather will help with every trigger. We conform even more to what we've written than with what we say.

Goals

We all conform to and are consistent with decisions and actions that help us achieve goals. Learning goals is easy—just ask!

Set up a safe "consistency zone" for your partner, one where he can make a relatively risk-free, comfortable decision. As always, do the hard work so that he doesn't have to. Help him avoid the pain of cognitive thinking. The consistency trigger provides a safe haven from sifting through data and logic. Ask what your partner's criteria will be to make the decision you seek. When he's finished, say, "If I can meet that criteria, can we go forward?" Meet the criteria and he'll be consistent with his prior statement.

We make powerful use of the consistency trigger when marketing our training programs. We always show that similar companies have bought, are using, and are benefiting from similar purchases. We show a list of 267 client companies including General Motors, Sony, Prudential, and Citigroup. It doesn't take much cognitive hard thinking to feel comfortable buying the same programs that these companies purchased.

Similarly, if we're working with a small company we show how hundreds of small company clients benefit. The prospect can seem very safe when conforming to what their respected peers did. This concept of showing how others acted is easily accomplished. Show that others have benefited from a similar idea. Get endorsements for your concept from people your partner will respect. Notice how authors promote their books—look at any current book to see the endorsements on the back cover and prior to the first chapter. When you tell your partner about your successes, he'll want to be consistent with that success.

Managers are highly motivated by the consistency trigger. Some of the best-selling management books are written by people we'd love to be consistent with. Books by Bill Gates, Lee Iacocca, and Jack Welch hit the best-seller lists quickly. Why? Maybe we can learn a few tidbits to be more consistent with these business giants.

CONSISTENCY PAYS OFF!

Why is it five times easier to persuade an existing client than a prospect? Because people need to be consistent with prior actions. If they've done business with the company before, they're five times more likely to be consistent with that relationship than when creating a new one. No hard thinking, easier decision.

Our need for consistency is a treasure trove for you. You can easily leverage consistency in your favor. Author Cavett Roberts understands consistency, saying, "People are more persuaded by the actions of others than by any proof we can offer." Show how others have benefited from actions similar to those you're proposing. Sir Joshua Reynolds put the choice of thinking versus automatic decisions simply: "There is no expedient to which a man will not resort to avoid the real labor of thinking." The savvy persuader will help his partner avoid that labor.

Because we're comfortable with our own past decisions and actions and comfortable with the actions of respected peers, applying the internal consistency trigger helps give us the sense of avoiding risk. When consistent with past actions and with peers, we significantly reduce risk. Persuade successfully by helping your partner reduce risk. Learn what your partner will be consistent with. Show how your proposition is in concert with his past actions, with others' opinions, and you'll eliminate the need for analytical thinking—and gain quick, automatic compliance.

REVIEW AND REFERENCE

- Our internal guidance system compels us to be consistent with the way we see ourselves and our admired peers. From birth, we create an internal databank of beliefs and past performance. We use these as an easy, safe, nonthinking guide to trigger decisions.

- Consistency is acting in concert with one's past experience, values, feelings, and perceptions. Being consistent with these experiences makes us comfortable and confident that we are making the right decision.
- Consistency is the internal trigger that motivates us to be and to act the same as those we positively relate to. We each have "reference groups" we look to for consistency and we work hard to be consistent with these groups.
- Our internal guidance system requires us to be consistent with two categories of expectations—our own, and those of our admired peers.
- Find out how your partner has acted in the past on issues like those being discussed. Learn what he values, believes in, takes pride in. Research how your partner acted in situations similar to what you're proposing. Once you have the requisite information, frame your request so that his positive decision will be consistent with past actions.
- Set up a safe "consistency zone" for your partner, one where she can make a relatively risk-free, comfortable decision. Ask what your partner's criteria will be to make the decision you seek. Then say, "If I can meet that criteria, can we go forward?" Meet the criteria and she'll be consistent with her prior statement.
- For your CPO, current persuasion opportunity, we have an interactive form to help determine the most persuasive elements for the consistency trigger. Go to www.seventriggers.com where you can select the applicable elements, make notes, and print them out.

Chapter 11

Reciprocity Trigger

eciprocity is a trigger you'll love. It's extremely easy to facilitate. It benefits everyone, and it works like a charm—with consistent, predictably positive results. Reciprocity is a powerful basic internal trigger that we all respond to willingly and automatically. Learn it. Employ it. With the persuasiveness of reciprocity, you'll more easily win the results you seek.

One of the strongest, most universal internal triggers is the law of giving and receiving. The *reciprocity trigger* has deep historical roots in human development. Social scientists have determined that virtually every human society shares the rule of reciprocity. And these scientists believe that we humans and our societies exist today only because our ancient ancestors learned to reciprocate. Long before the concept of money evolved, our ancestors traded, bartered, and exchanged goods, services, and food. They created a network of indebtedness that has been built into our psyche—into a process the amygdala responds to easily and unerringly.

GENEROSITY PAYS!

Reciprocity is the well-documented, universal psychological requirement to have the recipient of a gift give back something in return. Every time you provide a gift or service you create a debt that must be repaid. Every human society requires this quid pro quo.

138

You do something for me and I am morally, ethically, and psychologically required to provide some sort of payback. The concept is built into our limbic system and is triggered as invariably as the fight-or-flight syndrome; it's hardwired in the brain.

One reason the reciprocity trigger works so effectively is that it is an amygdala-based limbic response—automatic. We do not have to go to the prefrontal cortex to mentally evaluate what we should do—we know that we must do something in return. The debt is logged in; we must reciprocate. We usually do not even think through the motives for the gift—we don't do a lot of mental research to determine why it was given, how much time, energy, or effort it cost, what went on behind the gift or service selection. We simply provide something in return.

THE UBIQUITOUS TRIGGER

The reciprocity trigger is successfully used in every phase of human endeavor. Politics lives or dies on reciprocity. Businesses derive huge benefits from this trigger. Our personal lives depend on it more than we realize. Civilization wouldn't exist without it.

Entire businesses have been built on the documented results of the reciprocity trigger. What is the first thing the sales rep does at a home shopping party? Right! She gives everyone a gift. The indebtedness begins there, after which almost everyone buys something. The time share business provides the gift of a free resort weekend to get you to listen to a sales pitch. The recipients feel a debt of obligation, and the payback works remarkably well. Brokerage houses, law firms, and financial consultants give free seminars to get you involved with their services.

Hoping you'll reciprocate with a listing, Realtors offer homeowners a free market analysis. The "GWP—gift with purchase" concept is now used by virtually every major cosmetic company.

Why? It works. The founder of the Estee Lauder cosmetics company devised a brilliant concept that dynamically accelerated the growth of the company. Ms. Lauder personally created the "gift with purchase" idea where a separate gift was offered as a bonus for specific purchases. The gift was often valued higher than the required purchase. But guess what—because of the "debt" created by the gift, the buyer usually bought more than intended.

THRIVING ON RECIPROCITY

Nowhere is the reciprocity trigger more evident than in politics and government. Reciprocity greases the wheels of politics. "Pork barrel" legislation is enabled by reciprocity—you pass this appropriation for me and I'll pass the next one for you.

The White House is filled with gifts from foreign dignitaries and heads of state. Reciprocity is a time-honored, very practical way of ingratiating yourself to other politicians. Lyndon Johnson perfected the reciprocity trigger to its highest level. Though not known as an intellectual, Johnson knew how to amass a treasure trove of outstanding IOUs and used them to gain and maintain his power base. He did for others, then redeemed the debts as he needed them. Reciprocity was Johnson's currency for power. Lobbyists, applying the reciprocity trigger to facilitate all kinds of legislation, make the reciprocity trigger a way of political life. They provide legislators with funds for "fact-finding" foreign trips and other gifts we seldom learn about. Charities send us small gifts— colorful stamps, address labels, calendars, and such to create a feeling of indebtedness. Statistically these small gifts increase the response rate by more than 100 percent. We often overpay when responding to a gift given us. We get a VFW poppy costing merely a few cents and give back a dollar or two. We accept a weekend vacation valued at several hundred dollars and purchase a $20,000 time share.

Willy Theisen, founder of the Godfather's pizza chain, gave Art Sobczak, owner of BusinessByPhone.Inc. a $3 bottle of Famous Dave's Devil's Spit Spicy Sauce while Art was waiting for a pizza. How did Art reciprocate? He sent the story to his 21,000 newsletter subscribers and included the Godfather's web address in case anyone was interested in a franchise. Not a bad payback for a $3 bottle of sauce.

WHEN NOTHING ELSE WORKS

Reciprocity often works when nothing else can. It is virtually impossible for us to reach top executives of major companies to discuss training opportunities. It just doesn't happen.

We came up with a unique idea. I found a bunch of antique magazines with advertising from ages gone by. We took these ads from the early 1900s and had them multi-matted, then framed into beautiful pieces of art that an executive would be proud to place in an office setting. We had a special letter written describing the difference between old and new advertising and made the same analogy with training. Everything was then packaged into a custom gift box. We sent the framed ads to targeted executives and then followed up with phone calls. In some cases we received "thank you" calls before we even made our calls. By phone, we reached literally every executive who received the gift. We made appointments and personally met with every single executive we wanted to see. A 100 percent success rate! And we're talking about companies the size of AT&T, American Standard, Gillette, and Citigroup. There is absolutely no way we could have reached these people without the reciprocity trigger. We gave—we got!

How strong is the reciprocity trigger? It is so powerful, so predictable, that many companies don't allow their employees to accept gifts. In fact we had one of our pictures returned, with thanks, for that reason. Why do companies forbid gift-taking? Because they know the reciprocity trigger works. Obviously they know that the recipient might give something in return—something that might not be in the company's best interest.

Wal-Mart is a prime example of the nongift policy. The company will not even allow its buyers to enjoy a meal with a vendor unless the Wal-Mart buyer picks up the tab. The company doesn't want its buyers to feel indebted to any vendor or to make any special deals to reciprocate for indebtedness.

We know the reciprocity trigger has been in evidence since the dawn of civilized society. It has been applied since then, even though we didn't know how the brain processed this information. All we had was anecdotal evidence and a hit-or-miss approach to applying the trigger.

Reciprocity is an internal trigger that simply cannot be denied. We now know how the trigger works and how the brain makes an immediate, nonevaluative, nonjudgmental response to a gift.

SIMPLE PROCESS; GREAT RESULTS!

How do you apply this marvelous, powerful, automatic trigger to facilitate the persuasion process? It's simple. Though, as with every trigger, success requires a bit of planning. Ask yourself, "What can I give the person I'm dealing with? What gift will be appropriate, appreciated and will generate the 'give back' response?" Jot down all of the possible answers and then determine what might work best.

TRIGGER ELEMENTS

The potential for activating the reciprocity trigger is infinite. Use your imagination, then good judgment regarding the best approach. Here are a few ideas for your planning process.

Physical
- Any physical gift
- Flowers
- Candy
- Product samples
- Corporate promotional gifts
- Book

Entertainment
- Show or sports tickets
- Golf outing
- Gift certificate

Information
- Consultation
- Tips and suggestions
- Articles, documents
- Helpful Web site URLs
- New industry data
- Competitive data
- Topic information

Compliments
- Praise
- A sincere compliment
- Your time
- Thanks!

- Birthday and anniversary remembrance
- "Public" accolade

Business

- Time off
- Travel
- Involvement in desired project
- Lunch or dinner
- Bonus
- Promotion
- Staff support
- Increased budget
- Award or recognition
- Special study
- Fund project
- A concession

Your gift can of course be a physical item—flowers sent by a local florist, items you know the other person will appreciate. Virtually anything appropriate to that individual will generate the reciprocity response. Do you have to provide a physical gift? Not at all. As noted, meals—lunches and dinners—are time-honored ways for giving and for creating a need to reciprocate.

Taking a client, friend, or associate for a golf outing, to a sports event, to the theater, are standard methods for creating a debt to be repaid. How about a service? Can you provide information? A helpful bit of advice? Some competitive data? Counseling or consulting? Can you offer a concession to start the conversation? Why not send someone news or magazine clips about subjects of interest—or links to Web sites that carry information your partner will benefit from. How about free web greeting cards for specific occasions? The gift of praise for an accomplishment or a job well done will always be well received, remembered, and reciprocated.

The secret to creating a psychological debt is to use every opportunity to benefit from the reciprocity trigger. Apply gifts of any type and if the "favor" is not returned immediately, you are building up IOUs that can be called in at will. Before any get-together with your partner make a thorough written list of all the goods, services, and information you might bring to this person. Then determine which gift or gifts are most appropriate for the occasion. Yes, this is work—but especially productive work. Perceived indebtedness will often get things done that nothing else can accomplish.

BE A GIFT GIVER AND REAP THE BENEFITS

Author Ralph Marston sets the stage for you with his suggestion, "Give everyone a gift. It wouldn't have to be a material gift, but it could be. It could be the gift of your undivided attention, a kind word, a smile, or a helping hand." And "everyone" includes the gatekeepers. The reciprocity trigger can help get you to people you could never access by yourself. Another author, Og Mandino, offers sage wisdom for the best gift you can bestow on anyone: "I will smile at friend and foe alike and make every effort to find in him or her, a quality to praise, now that I realize that the deepest yearning of human nature is the craving to be appreciated."

We yearn for attention and appreciation and we reciprocate handsomely when someone provides those gifts.

Reciprocity is the internal trigger that will bring you many of life's gifts.

REVIEW AND REFERENCE

- Reciprocity is the well-documented, universal psychological compulsion of the recipient of a gift to give back something in return. Every time you provide a gift or service you create a debt that must be repaid. Every human society requires this quid pro quo.
- The reciprocity trigger is successfully used in every phase of human endeavor. Politics lives or dies on reciprocity. Businesses derive huge benefits from this trigger. Our personal lives depend on it more than we realize. Civilization wouldn't exist without it.
- The secret to creating a psychological debt is to use every opportunity to benefit from the reciprocity trigger. Apply gifts of any type. Even if the gift is not immediately reciprocated, you are building IOUs to be called at will.
- Before any get-together with your partner make a thorough written list of all the goods, services, and information you might bring to this person. Then determine which gift or gifts are most appropriate. Perceived indebtedness will often get things done that nothing else can accomplish.
- For your CPO, current persuasion opportunity, we have an interactive form to help determine the most persuasive elements for the reciprocity trigger. Go to www.seventriggers.com where you can select the applicable elements, make notes, and print them out.

Chapter 12

Contrast Trigger

The *contrast trigger* is not only effective, it's fun to use. And properly applied, it's extremely successful. By fully understanding the contrast trigger you'll be able to frame your request for action in a highly specific, very effective manner. Do the work, frame your request well, and agreement is virtually automatic.

SHOW THE DIFFERENCE!

Scientists have assembled a vast array of research on the contrast trigger. This scientifically based information helps us get what we want from others. We accomplish our goals by getting our partner to see that our proposition is better than other alternatives. Proper framing of contrasts enables people to see that one approach is infinitely more desirable than another. The choice differences are real, but the perception of magnitude between two choices is totally dependent on the established base, the starting point. Put simply, our proposal looks like a sure winner when we communicate the right comparisons.

The scientific data is a bit . . . well, scientific, so I'll try to put them in layman's terms. The way we judge something, the way we make a decision pro or con, the way we act—it's all based on what we are comparing that decision to. The comparison might be to other alternatives or to doing nothing. Research shows that we make these comparative decisions as a response to all stimuli, both physical and psychological. Most every evaluative judgment, even beliefs and attitudes, is based on our frame of reference, our perceived base. Scientists refer to this frame of reference as the "adaptation level." In simple terms, the adaptation level is "where we are now." All judgments are relative to the adaptation level.

If, for example, you placed your hand in a bucket of cold water the adaptation level for that hand eventually becomes cold. If you removed your hand from the cold water and place it into a second bucket containing room-temperature water, the water in the second bucket seems warmer than it actually is. Adaptation changes one's perception. In this case, your hand adapts to the cold. Reality or logic (e.g., the actual temperature of the warmer water) has little bearing on the perceived temperature. The judgment of all stimuli, yes, both physical and psychological, is directly affected by the adaptation level. This is your key to persuasion by contrast.

Hold a heavy weight for a few minutes. Then pick up a lighter weight—it will feel lighter than it really is. This is why a batter swings a weighted bat before getting up to the plate. After the weighted bat the real one feels like a broomstick and he can swing it faster, more easily. Look at a bright light for a while and a lesser light will seem even dimmer than it is. The comparative list is endless, infinite, and it's automatically defined by our brain.

OBJECTIVE VALUES DON'T MATTER

Clinical psychologists who research adaptation level phenomena have determined that the human brain responds to the *relativity* of stimuli, *not to the objective values of the stimuli*. Please check this sentence again—it's critically important to your persuasion efforts. Perhaps this is one reason why logic, reason, and cognitive thought play lesser roles in our decision-making process than previously thought. Perceptions guide our decisions and our actions even when perceptions have little concern with fact or reality. Perhaps this explains the truism that "perception is reality." Facts, logic, and reality clearly take a back seat to adaptive level comparisons and perceptions.

While I was studying psychology at Lafayette College, our class often took lab trips to Princeton University to work in their psychology labs. Princeton has an extraordinary facility showing how perceptions defy logic and reality. In short, based on the setup, the construction of the adaptation level, we see things that are perceived differently than they really are. For example, rooms were built with ceiling and wall lines that appeared to make the room smaller at one end—so small that you actually ducked when walking through them. The perception was an illusion. These trips were exciting revelations into the real world—not as it is but as we perceive it to be.

THE SETUP—ADAPTING FOR SUCCESS!

So what does one's perspective have to do with persuasion, the process of getting the action you want with and through others? Everything! The way you set up the adaptation level, the way you frame your communication, the order in which you make your points, will determine your success or failure.

Let's say you require capital funding for a project that could be accomplished in either of two ways. Let's assume one option costs considerably more than another. You want approval on the less costly approach and want the lesser budget authorized. Since you have two options, you can give the boss and the bean counters a choice. When you meet with the boss, how will you frame your request? Which option will you present first? Right! The most expensive. The most time- and resource-consuming options should be presented first. Why? Because you are setting the adaptation level. Set the level high and the second option will be not only less costly than the first, but it will appear even less costly than it actually is. Properly framed it will look like a bargain and you'll have a much greater chance for the approval you seek.

If you were a Realtor, would you show several houses at the upper end of the customer's price range first or last? Same answer. Smart Realtors set the adaptation level, then show lesser priced options. Why? Because by comparison to the adaptation level the lower priced houses are perceived to be even more of a bargain than they actually are. How do savvy marketers benefit from the concept? When would you present the shirt, tie, and shoe purchases to a suit buyer? Before or after the suit purchase? Many believe getting easier, less expensive items agreed to first will benefit the overall sale. Not so. By the time the customer has spent $600 on the suit, the $55 shirt seems relatively inexpensive. The $35 tie is downright cheap.

If anyone told me I would ever pay $1,300 for a car CD changer stereo system, I would have said they were crazy. Yet after parting with mega-bucks for a car, the high-end JBL system with the powered bass amplifier and the 10-CD changer seemed like peanuts compared to the car cost. In retrospect the amount spent was ludicrous; yet at the time my adaptation level was in full control.

Many businesses offer different costs for different volumes of products. Volume discounts are part and parcel of virtually every commodity, wholesale or retail. What's the best way to take advantage of the contrast trigger? What's the best way to set the adaptation level so your offer appears irresistible? It's simple.

Rather than offering the best volume price up front, show the cost if your partner were paying on an individual unit basis. Multiply the number of units times the unit price and show the number. Put it in writing. Set the adaptation level. It will be, should be unrealistically high. Then show your best discounted price. The comparison will appear better than if you showed this up front. More important, the partner can take both prices to the bean counters and show how much she is saving the company through shrewd bargaining.

WHAT GOES FIRST?

How then do you benefit from this solid, highly reliable internal contrast trigger? The framing of your proposal, your order of communication, is critical. The bottom line, the "scientific take-away," from comparative and adaptation studies, is that all types of stimuli can be arranged in some meaningful order. Your challenge is to arrange your stimuli, your communication, to take best advantage of the comparison trigger.

Temperatures can be arranged from hot to cold, weights from heavy to light or vice versa. Perceptions and attitudes can be arranged from the most negative to the most positive. Present an offer with all the bells and whistles, the most expensive, the most time consuming, the most complex, the most difficult approach to what you seek. Then present what you really want—in a simpler, easier to manage, and better-value framework. The comparison will be magnified to seem even more reasonable than it really is.

TRIGGER ELEMENTS

The key to activating the contrast trigger is to first set the adaptation level. The adaptation level should be set high, at the most costly, most time-consuming, most energy-demanding, most convoluted level. Then show how your approach is easier, quicker, safer, less costly, more practical than the adaptation level you set. When you set the adaptation level well, your approach will seem even more beneficial than it would appear without the comparison.

Here are several areas where you might set the adaptation levels for beneficial comparisons:

Cost comparisons
Easy! Create and show several options—highest cost first, replete with bells and whistles, followed by what you really want.

Time comparisons
Again—create options, show a lengthy, laborious approach, then your simple quick proposal.

Energy comparisons
If his own energy and personal input is a factor, show alternatives with different input requirements. Save the easiest for last.

Resource comparisons
Define the necessary resources—show the most involved, costly approach, then show yours, saving valuable resources.

Personal effort versus others doing it
Determine how you want the project to be done—position the easiest route for last.

Alternative comparisons—relativity
Whenever there are several ways to get it done, show the alternatives, the options, presenting the most onerous first, then the relatively easy approach you want. Compare and contrast the options to amplify the ease of your suggestion.

Seek options, compare
There are usually many approaches to reach the same result. Seek out the options, put them in the best order to set the adaptation level high, then wow her with the approach you want.

Show how your proposal is better than other options, different from the competition's, different from what others have proposed. Show that it is cheaper, easier, safer, less risky, better than other solutions proposed. Do the serious work—find the comparisons, then frame them in the best order. Learn where your partner is coming from, what his current adaptation level is relative to the subject under discussion. His current perceptions will define how readily he will react to your proposal. If he is risk-averse, show how your proposition will preclude risk. If he is concerned about money, mention that concern and then show how you will save money or generate more. If frightened, allay fear. If adventurous, show how this will be a wonderful new experience.

When you're physically hot, a cool stimulus to the skin is positive. When you are cold, that same cool stimulus will be a negative. Pour some cool water over your head during a hot summer jog and it feels refreshing. Now imagine doing the same thing during a mid-winter ski run. You get the idea. When you frame your presentation in the right order, you magnify the differences and motivate the decisions you seek. Be certain your cool stimulus is applied to hot skin!

NOT EVEN A PRETENSE OF OBJECTIVITY

Our colleagues in the scientific community have done some marvelous work for us. They have documented that the brain, as it deals with contrasting situations, does not depend on "even a pretense of objectivity." They inform us that compared to perception, logic and reason play a very diminished role. Comparisons are magnified as they vary from the adaptation level.

Taken individually, the contrast trigger and its relationship to perception and persuasion appear to be a simple concept; but included in the overall context of how we motivate decisions and generate actions in others, we recognize that this concept has a profound influence on all human interaction. The new scientific revelations of perception, contrast, and brain function override all potential value of logic and cognitive evaluation.

The knowledge that science has documented now allows us to set the stage to facilitate the results we seek from others by utilizing their own internal navigation systems, their internal triggers, their own perception of reality. To the human brain, reality is always what we perceive it to be. Work with the brain, with your partner's realities, to succeed at your persuasion goals.

REVIEW AND REFERENCE

- We accomplish our goals by showing that our proposition is better than alternatives. Proper framing of contrasts enables people to see that one approach is infinitely more desirable than another. The choice differences are real, but the perception of magnitude between two choices is totally dependent on the established base, the starting point. Put simply, our proposal looks like a sure winner when we communicate the right comparisons.
- Adaptation level is the key. Most every evaluative judgment is based on our frame of reference, or adaptation level. All judgments are relative to the adaptation level.
- The framing of your proposal, your order of communication, is critical. Your challenge is to arrange your communication to take best advantage of the comparison trigger. Always present the most onerous approach first, then what you really want.
- Show how your proposal is better than other options, different from the competition's, different from what others have proposed. If he is risk-averse, show how your proposition will preclude risk. If he is concerned about money, mention that concern and then show how you will save money or generate more. If

frightened, allay fear. If adventurous, show how this will be a wonderful new experience.

- When you frame your presentation in the right order, you magnify the differences and motivate the decisions you seek.
- For your CPO, current persuasion opportunity, we have an interactive form to help determine the most persuasive elements for the contrast trigger. Go to www.seventriggers.com where you can select the applicable elements, make notes, and print them out.

Chapter 13

Reason Why Trigger

W ould you like a simple, very easy way to get quick, nonthinking compliance? Give your partner a reason why he should do what you seek. That's it! Pure and simple. And—as the documentation shows—it works!

The *reason why* trigger works well because the amygdala seems to accept a valid reason and doesn't bother to send the information to the cerebral cortex for thoughtful, rational evaluation. The amygdala OKs the reason as a shortcut to avoid heavy thinking, and you get compliance.

The reason why trigger has been successfully applied for ages. However, since it was a hit-or-miss anecdotal approach, we didn't develop the awareness of amygdala-cortex interaction until recently.

There's a surprising volume of scientific research into the reason why trigger. Long before anyone knew how brain paths worked, academics created situations to test the concept. They would construct situations where someone was asked to do something—say, break into a line of people waiting to accomplish a task. When asked, "Can I get ahead of you?" the answer was generally "No!" But given a reason, such as, "I'm double parked" or "My meter is running out—can I get in front of you?" the answer would invariably be "OK." The amygdala simply accepted the reason and the request received immediate, nonthinking compliance. Many studies in this arena document similar results—ask without a reason, get turned down; provide a reason, persuade successfully. Today we can apply this trigger with certainty, and with predictable results. We know we can persuade decisions and actions simply by giving others a good reason to do what we want.

GIVE A REASON, GAIN COMPLIANCE!

The reason why can be virtually any reason the other person can accept. It can be your reason or his. Anything that makes even a little sense to your partner will work.

Marketers and retailers have long known the results of the reason why trigger, though they didn't have a clue as to how it worked. They use "going out of business" or "lost our lease" or "overstocked merchandise" as reasons why we should shop their wares. We bite.

"You get what you pay for" is a reason we all use to justify buying high-priced items. The reason we spend big bucks for some items is because we equate price with quality—remember the Opium perfume example? We are conditioned to accept the high price reason to get high quality.

Scarcity is an excellent example of a reason why. When availability is limited for something we want or need, motivation to act is accelerated. We treasure exclusivity, rarity, uniqueness, and we act quickly when these opportunities arise. Scarcity includes an insufficient supply, and a blockbuster reason why—limited time. We are absolute pushovers when things have a time limit associated with them. When something we want is limited to a time window, we tend to act more quickly. This trigger works because we perceive a chance to miss the deal if we don't act.

Wine pricing is based on the scarcity aspect of the reason why trigger. When a good appellation vintage has limited availability, the price point is high. Conversely, even a well-crafted *Côtes du Rhône* does not command a high price. Good as it is, it's ubiquitous and always in ample supply. Scarcity alone often creates value and motivates action.

The exclusivity factor of the reason why trigger is powerful. A limited edition, a collectible, a short production run, a one-of-a-kind item, these are all strong motivators causing us to act, often without much rational thought.

When original papers and drawings of Leonardo Da Vinci were offered at auction, "the one-and-only" scarcity aspect of the reason why trigger prevailed, as did Bill Gates who kept bidding until he won the prize.

Scarcity, even presumed scarcity, motivates action. In Prince Georges County, Maryland, in all of 2003, the health department received 2,700 calls requesting information about flu shots. In 2004, the year of the presumed (but inaccurate) flu shot shortage, the same department received 20,400 calls in October alone!

Good Realtors are great at applying the reason why trigger. They come up with all kinds of reasons why we should buy, and buy now.

While looking at houses on the Eastern Shore of Maryland, we virtually discounted one house. Logic and reason told us there were too many problems. There was no dock, the water depth was insufficient for the boat, necessary alteration variances were virtually impossible to obtain, the septic system was questionable, the roof needed replacement, and a good deal of other work was needed. It didn't even have a functional kitchen.

On our second visit, the skilled Realtor gave a reason why we should proceed if we were interested. On Saturday, another couple was coming from Pennsylvania for their third look-see. They were obviously very interested and close to buying. The reason why hijacked all our logic. We bought the house on Friday. Had I used logic and reason, I never would have bought this property. And I would have missed out on an almost 100 percent increase in value in only two years.

At ProEd, we apply the reason why trigger very effectively. With this trigger, I persuaded a client to pre-pay a six-figure amount for a program they were not going to need for many months. The reason? "I need some extra cash because I am buying my partners out." It worked. We got a check. And the client got a reduced price for the license.

In another instance, we combined the reason why with "timing" as a second reason. We told the potential client that we would offer a very special deal (it was) because we were financing the marketing of a new training program. Totally true. We then added that the special offer would only hold for a month, since by that time the marketing would be done. We got the contract immediately.

Another client was dragging its corporate heels on the decision to proceed with a contract we knew they wanted. Negotiations were limping along for almost a year. I gave them a reason to make a decision. The offer I originally made was good for only one more month, as our financing for still another program was almost complete. After that their cost would go from $110,000 to regular pricing of $150,000. A good reason why to act! We got a check for $110,000 in a week and the client saved $40,000.

Sometimes I'm quite surprised at how effective the reason why trigger can be. I had been attempting to get an appointment with an executive of a West Coast company for over nine months. He turned down every attempt to get together for a presentation, stating that, among other reasons, he didn't yet have the decision maker in place for the issues under consideration.

I had a speaking engagement in Honolulu and realized I might have a good reason why to employ to possibly get an appointment. I called and told him I was going to stop in Los Angeles on the way back to New York, so why not get together for just a few minutes to share some ideas. He agreed, and only because I was going to be there anyway. I quickly changed my flight arrangements to stop over in L.A., booked a hotel room, a car, and set up the meeting with him and his staff. We met, and I left with a $65,000 contract! Without the reason why trigger, I'd still be trying to get an appointment with this guy.

A GOOD REASON *MAKES* THE DIFFERENCE!

Applying the reason why trigger is really easy. Just do the up-front work. As always, do the hard work and your partner will not have to. Write out a list of reasons why your partner should do what you want. List honest, plausible reasons why he should act now rather than later. Then present your reasons. Perhaps the project cost will be higher later. Resources might be available for a specific time window. Stretch your imagination to list ways your idea, product, project, or proposal is unique, rare, limited, or has time limitations. Put limits on your own availability or support. "The reason we need to do this now is because I'll be unavailable—out of the country—after this month."

When the amygdala OKs a trigger, it acts quickly without feedback from the cerebral cortex. Any acceptable reason why will activate the trigger to accept your proposal.

TRIGGER ELEMENTS

Here are several reason why items to consider as you plan your meeting.

Cost

Get what you pay for. Provide a good reason why your proposal is higher in price than others—use the price/value equation to set up the reason why.

Limited pricing

Trite as it sounds, when the price is limited by availability, time, or any other factor, tell it like it is. The amygdala will accept a good reason.

Time issues—infinite number

Any and all timing issues are viable ways to activate the reason why trigger. Of course you can set your own time limits—on your availability, on the deal terms, on the project.

Limited supply

If your proposal involves anything that is or can be construed to be in limited supply, say so. Any way you can show that limits are a good reason to act will help.

Impending event

An event that will stop or slow down the process you seek can be a good reason to proceed now. You can usually find impending events that will activate the reason why trigger.

Exclusivity or rarity

Establish the rarity or exclusivity of any element of your proposal, as a reason why she should act now. Make the proposition exclusive to your partner for a limited time, and you have a double reason why.

Team support

"As a team member, you can appreciate how this will help the team and the organization."

Possible advancement within the organization

If successful completion of the opportunity you suggest might lead to advancement within the company, present this as a great reason why your partner should act.

> ### Contest
>
> If you're in sales or marketing, contests are a hugely successful reason why your partner should act now. Telling someone you need just "x, y, or z" to earn a trip or prize often activates the reason why trigger. This one is magic!
>
> ### New information
>
> When you can't get to see someone you want to persuade, you need a reason why. A great reason why is "I've just received some new information I know you'll find interesting. Let's get together and I'll share it with you."

GIVE THE REASON, GET THE DECISION

The advertising guru who founded the Book of the Month plan provides sage advice: "Whenever you make a claim or special offer, come up with an honest reason why and state it sincerely." You will be much more successful in your persuasion attempts.

The reason why trigger is fundamental to our decision process. Why? Because it motivates our inherent need for amygdala-based, nonthinking shortcuts to avoid the time, energy, and pain for complex thinking. Do the work. Think through the reasons that will apply to your partner and the current situation. Make the reason why trigger fundamental to your persuasion attempts. Present the reason, and get the decision you seek.

REVIEW AND REFERENCE

- The reason why trigger works well because the amygdala seems to accept any valid reason and doesn't bother to send the information to the cerebral cortex. The amygdala OKs the reason as a shortcut to avoid heavy thinking, and you get compliance.

- Many studies document the following: ask without a reason, get turned down; provide a reason, persuade successfully.
- The reason why can be virtually any reason the other person can accept. It can be your reason or theirs. Anything that makes even a little sense to your partner will work.
- Scarcity is an excellent example of a reason why. When availability is limited for something we want or need, motivation to act is accelerated. This trigger works because we perceive a chance to miss the deal if we don't act.
- Applying the reason why trigger is easy. Just do the up-front work. Write out a list of reasons why your partner should do what you want. Include your own reasons. List honest, plausible reasons why he should act now rather than later.
- For your CPO, current persuasion opportunity, we have an interactive form to help determine the most persuasive elements for the reason why trigger. Go to www.seventriggers.com where you can select the applicable elements, make notes, and print them out.

Chapter 14

Hope Trigger

HOPES AND DREAMS RULE OUR INTERNAL TRIGGERS

What is a prime driver for your own personal decisions and actions? Isn't it the quest for the things that you want and hope for? What you want to have? What you want to do? What you hope to be? You hope for what you want, and hope that the wrong things do not happen. Hope motivates virtually all human activity. One of the dominating factors in our lives, hope is a powerhouse internal trigger that automatically helps determine our decisions and our actions.

Savvy persuaders understand the compelling nature of the hope trigger and apply it to motivate desired action. Charles Revson, the legendary founder of the giant Revlon Corporation and a genius at persuasion, built his dynasty on a single concept, which he stated in very simple terms: "In the factory we make cosmetics. In the store, we sell hope."

Acquire the skills to successfully employ the hope trigger and you might be as successful a persuader and leader as Revson. The good news—hope is one of the easiest internal triggers to activate. We are easily persuaded by those who understand our hopes, our wishes, our dreams, and by those who help us to realize our desires.

Hope is a combination of wishes and positive expectations. Its power is unmatched in persuasive ability. The key to this formidable trigger is simplicity itself. Learn what people hope for. Then frame your proposal to help them meet those hopes.

Hope is our fundamental internal trigger. Against all logic, reason, and common sense, we are persuaded to follow and act on our hopes and dreams. We live our entire lives employing mental shortcuts just so that we might realize those hopes and dreams. Most important, we are easily—yes, outrageously—persuaded by those who understand our hopes and provide us with a means to achieve them. Tap into the hope trigger and you'll be a highly successful persuader. You'll gain the compliance and results you might not achieve any other way.

Virtually every persuasion decision is based to some degree on the hope trigger, the persuader that underlies all others. We hope our decisions and actions will somehow improve our lives, our status, help us become more successful, make our lives easier, and, yes, the biggest hope of all—make us happy. This trigger is such a powerful motivator that once we perceive an opportunity to satisfy our hopes we seldom rely on rational cognitive thought, on logic, before we act. Rather than engaging laborious thinking, we make quick, automatic, amygdala-based shortcut decisions. Our internal trigger is activated. With high hopes, we go for it!

The constant, always present desire for happiness is the gut-level foundation for the omnipotent hope trigger. The things we hope for determine the decisions and actions we make.

HOPE VERSUS LOGIC

You see startling, nonthinking, automatic activation of the hope trigger all day, every day. One of the best examples is the hope for instant happiness through instant riches. The hugely successful state and interstate lotteries thrive on the hope trigger. The chances of winning a lottery are staggeringly low. Not a shred of logic or reason is employed to weigh the odds. Statistically you are more likely to be killed by lightning on the way to the lottery vendor than you are likely to win the big prize. Rationally the lottery is a waste of money. It's a tax. Yet we plunk down our hard-earned dollars based on nothing but hope. Does logical, evaluative thought stop anyone? Against all reason, logic, and cognitive thought, we line up at the machines to print out our ticket to happiness. Logic and reason? Not a chance! Hope wins!

Las Vegas, Atlantic City, Monaco, and the like were built entirely on the hope trigger. We go to the casinos oblivious that logic dictates that the only long-term winners are casino operators and their shareholders. Does this deter gamblers? Do we care that, logically, a large percentage of the money we gamble goes to the casino and little is returned to us? Is the money spent at the casino a good, sound, well-reasoned investment? Of course not. But the hope trigger, the amygdala, trumps all reason. The amygdala doesn't even make a pretense of sending the information to the prefrontal cortex for cognitive evaluation. We want to have fun, to be happy and well. We think we'll probably win, and we act.

The vitamin and, yes, even much of the pharmaceutical industry is built on hope. We buy vitamins and over-the-counter medications in the hope that we'll feel better, look better, and live longer, happier lives.

How many doctors really do the heavy lifting to verify the research data, side effects, potential interactions, stats and efficacy documentation of the medications they prescribe? Or do these doctors merely accept the ethos—the authority of the drug companies and their research and just *hope* the drugs will work as promoted? Don't we hope for the same promised results without doing the difficult work of pharmaceutical research? We hope the pharmaceutical company and the doctor are right.

What triggers were so effectively employed by Jack Welch when he created the stunning turnaround at General Electric? He went to virtually every operating division in every part of the world and gave managers and workers a single message—a message that became his mantra. That mantra included no message that required logic or cognitive thought. It included no message about the data, facts and figures on the finances or growth of the GE empire. His message—designed to reach the amygdala of every GE worker—was simply this: "Every G.E. unit that is not #1 or #2 in its industry will be either fixed, sold, or closed."

On hearing this mantra pronounced, what do you think the hundreds of thousands of GE employees hoped for? Right! They hoped to keep their jobs! They hoped to achieve the goals Welch set out. Employing their own internal guidance systems, the hope trigger performed miracles; miracles no amount of data, logic, or reasoning could achieve. Welch's ethos—his authority trigger—made the mantra believable and acceptable. The hope trigger, reinforced with authority, helped make GE what it is today.

Trump employed the friendship trigger to position himself with the right people to execute his visions. Yet it was the hope trigger that persuaded the New York politicians and the financial community to agree to his plans. Each person and group that he persuaded hoped to achieve the results Trump outlined. Trump researched what people hoped for—then tapped into the partners' internal guidance systems to execute his goals.

Iacocca employed the authority, friendship, and hope triggers to accomplish many of his extraordinary feats. Certainly the hope trigger worked beautifully with a Congress that hoped not to lose an American icon to bankruptcy and possible annihilation.

My company, and indeed the entire training industry, builds its foundation on the hope trigger. Do you hope for better sales? Then conduct a sales training program. Do you hope for better customer relations? Better implement a customer service representative training program. Do you hope for better management results? You get the idea.

Overall, the hope of business is that with good training, results will improve. The logic is that with good training and with good management and leadership follow-up, performance increases will happen.

Where possible, we insist that management go through the same training as their staff. Logic and reason dictate that this is the only way they will know which activities to manage. It's the only way training will produce the results the companies hope for. Yet many companies simply provide staff training and hope for the results. As usual, hope wins over reason.

LEARN YOUR PARTNER'S HOPES

As already noted, the internal hope trigger is easy to facilitate. And when you learn how to determine what people hope for, it's easy to position your presentation to address those hopes. How do you learn what your partner hopes for? Ask!

In our training programs we offer participants a process called "value profiling." This is a questioning technique designed to get your partner to share information regarding the hopes and end results he wants regarding the current issue. We'll share more about value profiling in the communications chapter, but put simply, you ask and you listen. Ask several questions to learn your partner's hopes, goals, and desired outcomes for the subject at issue. The questions might include short-term hopes, long-term goals, business hopes, and personal interests. Questions often focus on minimum expectations and "best of all worlds" solutions. Make questions specific to the proposal.

TRIGGER ELEMENTS

Here are items you might question your partner about—the answers will help you activate her hope trigger.

Happiness

The unending quest for happiness is perhaps the biggest of all human hopes. We're hardwired to accept any approach that even remotely enhances our happiness. When you show how your proposition will produce positive feelings, you've activated the hope trigger. "Think about how good you'll feel when we finish this deal."

More time

We hope for more time and hope to accomplish more in the time we have. Show how your proposition will save time and accomplish more.

Health

A critical hope motivator. Each of us hopes to stay or get more healthy. Find ways to align your idea with this hope. "Taking this approach is sure to lower your stress—it'll solve all those outstanding issues."

Independence

Most who feel trapped, hope for a degree of independence. If your idea can help achieve that hope, put it in those terms. "This process will create the independence you seek in the purchasing arena."

Goals and ambitions

Professional goals drive many lives. Ask, and people will readily tell you their goals. Then activate the hope trigger showing how your plan will accelerate achieving the hoped-for goals.

Fears

What does she want *not* to happen? Fear is a mega-motivator. We each hope specific fears just will not occur. Learn what she hopes to avoid, then show how you can support that hope.

Success
Like happiness, we hope for success in business and in our personal lives. Ask the right questions, and your partner will be delighted to share the hopes and dreams he has for success. You can then easily activate the internal hope trigger.

Profit
We all hope for profit—from our business, from our investments, from our activities. Profit is a strong element for the hope trigger. When you show how your partner will profit—financially, emotionally, socially, in business and at home—you have fully engaged the hope trigger.

Avoid loss
Like fear, loss avoidance is a big hope. Learn what she might hope to avoid losing, and show what you can do to help.

Achievement
If your partner hopes to achieve specific objectives, tap into that hope. It's a key to the hope trigger.

Promotion
Another hope most have. If you can help achieve that hope, show how.

Fame or notoriety
Ego is another powerful hope. If your partner hopes for ego reinforcement, give it! You'll reap great rewards.

Stability
Ours is a chaotic, volatile world. We hope for calm and stability. When you're dealing with an issue that will introduce calm and stability, activate the hope trigger. Let your partner know your approach will smooth things out.

Peer acceptance
We hope for peer acceptance almost as much as we hope for happiness. We hope to look good, and to be well-thought-of by our peers. Show how your approach will make her look good to her peers, and the hope trigger will kick in automatically.

Brainstorm questions before you get together, then present them when you do. You can then frame your communication to show how your proposal will help meet their hopes. Value profiling is easy, fun, and profitable because people love to talk about themselves. They will gladly expound on their hopes, dreams, and fears. The information they provide is just what you need to quickly and easily point them in the right decision.

In making your proposal, the key is not to simply make the right points, but to tie them into the hopes and wishes uncovered. One further point. Never, ever, expect your partner to make the tie-in between your proposal and how it will benefit him. Often he won't make the connection and certainly he won't make it as clearly as you can.

We find this inability for persuaders to connect the dots to be a huge failing in persuasive presentations. The presenter thinks, "Well this is easy to understand—of course he'll make the tie-in." Doesn't happen! You have to draw the lines in for your partner. While the hope trigger commands automatic decisions and action, people are concerned with the outcomes of their decisions. Only when you learn what they hope for, and what they seek to avoid, can you successfully apply this trigger. Consequences motivate behavior. Be sure you explain how those consequences support the hopes and goals you have uncovered. We either take or avoid certain actions because we perceive certain events or consequences will follow.

There are three easy-to-remember rules of consequences.

1. Consequences perceived to provide rewards motivate behavior and action.
2. Consequences perceived to be negative or punitive create negative decisions and behavior.
3. Consequences that deliver neither reward nor punishment create no behavior.

Keep these in mind. The potential for reward or punishment is a potent motivator. Be certain your presentation offers rewards in keeping with hopes and wishes. And make sure you mention any potential negative consequences that might occur if they do not act.

Like every other trigger, the hope trigger requires pre-work. As usual, you want to do the pre-work, to go through the pain of thinking, so your partner can avoid it and make an easy decision.

Combining the authority and consistency triggers with the hope trigger works wonders. When we learn a company wants to increase its business, we show how companies including Prudential, Citigroup, General Motors, Sony, and similar companies grew their businesses with our training and consulting programs. When a potential client sees a letter documenting a 26 percent business increase, or an 11.4 percent sales growth from a company with 4,234 reps, or a $3.8 million savings in hiring and training costs, that's credibility, authority. Understanding the credibility of your proposal, they can hope to be consistent in achieving the same results.

FIND THE INCENTIVE TO ACTION—YOUR PARTNER'S HOPES

Remember my question about your own motivation for personal decisions and actions? A compendium of research states that for 2,500 years, students of human nature have concluded that "pleasure drives the brain." We now know that the amygdala makes instant decisions when the brain perceives outcomes in concert with our hopes. With little or no evaluative thinking required, the thought process won't even be sent to the prefrontal cortex for evaluation.

Playwright and author Jean Kerr offers a clever comment on our hopes: "Hope is the feeling you have that the feeling you have isn't permanent." Activate the hope trigger by showing that the present isn't permanent—there is a better way.

A woman buys Revlon face cream in the hope of reducing the crow's feet around the eyes. A golfer orders a new driver in the hope it will give him more distance off the tee. Hope for a future benefit is a huge motivator to action. The realization of the hope is ephemeral—the wrinkles may or may not disappear. The distance off the tee may be into the rough. But hope is always there. Capture it!

My hope is simple—it's that you learn and apply one or more of the seven internal triggers to every interaction, every communication situation you encounter. As previously mentioned, there are an infinite number of triggers we have each built into our personal database. The seven internal triggers described here form the basis of how we make the majority of our decisions. They are real. They are documented to work. They allow you to work with your partner's brain and internal guidance system rather than against it.

These seven internal triggers will help you achieve your business, professional, and personal persuasion goals. Triggers will form the crux of your discussions. The information about the new brain science and the internal triggers is interesting, and yes, it's exciting. But you need more, much more than information to achieve the persuasion results you seek. Knowledge is wonderful, but we still have to execute.

REVIEW AND REFERENCE

- We are easily persuaded by those who understand our hopes, our wishes, our dreams, and by those who help us achieve them. Hope is a combination of wishes and positive expectations. Learn what people hope for. Then frame your proposal to help them meet those hopes.
- Against all logic, reason, and common sense, we are persuaded to follow and act on our hopes and dreams.
- Virtually every persuasion decision is based to some degree on the hope trigger. We hope our decisions and actions will somehow improve our lives, our status, help us become more successful, make our lives easier, and, yes, the biggest hope of

all—make us happy. Once we perceive an opportunity to satisfy our hopes we seldom rely on rational cognitive thought, on logic, before we act.

- The internal hope trigger is easy to facilitate. When you learn what people hope for, it's easy to position your presentation to address those hopes. Learning what your partner hopes for is simple. Just ask.
- List questions, then present them. Frame your communication to show how your proposal will help meet the hopes expressed. The key is not simply to make the right points, but to tie them into the hopes and wishes.
- We hope for the right consequences from our decisions and actions. Be sure you explain how those consequences support the hopes and goals you have uncovered. We either take or avoid certain actions because we perceive certain events or consequences will follow.
- There are three easy-to-remember rules of consequences.
  1. Consequences perceived to provide rewards motivate positive behavior and action.
  2. Consequences perceived to be negative or punitive create negative decisions and behavior.
  3. Consequences that deliver neither reward nor punishment create no behavior.
- The potential for reward or punishment is a potent motivator. Be certain your presentation offers rewards in keeping with hopes and wishes. And make sure you mention potential negative consequences if they do not act.
- For your CPO, current persuasion opportunity, we have an interactive form to help determine the most persuasive elements for the hope trigger. Go to www.seventriggers.com where you can select the applicable elements, make notes, and print them out.

Chapter 15

Persuasion Goals

You can have anything you want, but first you must know what you want.

Precisely, what do you want from a specific persuasion attempt? Sure, you know in general, yet can you state your end-game goal in clear, concise, detailed, specific terms? Can you measure your persuasion results against a well-defined, previously documented standard? Can you identify the cost—yours or others'—to achieve that goal? Does your persuasion goal have a specific time frame?

The next few chapters will deal with issues I have found in no other work about persuasion. These chapters will deal with the "How To" as well as the "What To" elements of the complete persuasion process. Learning how the brain processes information, and learning how we help trigger the actions we seek are important. But how do you best execute the process to get the compliance and results you seek?

Information is great, it's fun, and yes, it's interesting. But we want more than knowledge—we want results. So let's get into the mechanics for translating our new knowledge and information into tangible, desired persuasion results. Results depend on practical execution steps.

The first, absolutely crucial step to persuasion success is setting your goal and knowing precisely where you are headed. Perhaps football's legendary Hall of Fame quarterback Joe Namath put it best: "To be a leader, you have to make people want to follow you, and nobody wants to follow someone who doesn't know where he's going."

An unknown author put it even more succinctly, "There's no point in carrying the ball until you learn where the goal is."

Success, especially leadership success, is determined by setting specific goals and then persuading others to execute and reach those goals. Normally your business operational goals are well defined. We don't do nearly so well with our other goals. Your ability to set, then achieve, your persuasion goals will define your overall success.

By now you are probably saying, "Well sure, you have to know where you're going, and I do." Most people, most managers, believe they have good personal goals. They can cite them for you: "I want better support from my people." "I want to grow the business." "I want an increase in commissions." "I want you to do a better job." "I want a promotion." "I want to create an effective, positive change in my organization." "I want my people to execute more effectively. . . ."

In our lexicon, these are not goals. Not even close! They are dreams or wishes. They may be the results of goal achievement but they lack every criterion for a well-stated, achievable goal. A well-stated, achievable goal must have four elements.

1. A specific, measurable action.
2. A time limit or target date.
3. A cost estimate, stated in dollars, energy, or effort.
4. Identified resources, people, and/or material.

MAKE IT MEASURABLE

The most important of the four criteria is having a measurable standard. It is imperative that you have a clear goal to measure results against.

"I want to persuade a department manager to grow his business" sounds like a goal. Is quarterly growth of one-tenth of 1 percent OK? It's growth. You achieved the stated goal. No. A better statement of the goal might be, "I want to persuade this department manager to generate fourth-quarter growth of 7.5 percent over Q-4 last year." This is measurable. It is a firm goal against which you can check performance. It doesn't allow the mind to hedge—you make it or you don't. You persuaded your people to perform or you didn't.

You might want to persuade a manager to reduce department expenses through increased productivity and staff reduction. Is "reduced expenses" a measurable goal? Is any small expense reduction satisfactory? Of course not. Be specific. Request the actual target in concrete, measurable terms. Then both you and the person you're persuading know the standard to measure against actual performance.

How much time will you allow for your persuasion goal to be realized? Someday doesn't exist. Tomorrow never comes. Avoid the "someday" syndrome by setting specific time frames for both your partner meeting and the expected action. You now have achieved the second element, a measurable standard.

Setting goals for costs and resources is also important. Many times in our training and consulting work we have executives go through this four-step process in real terms for real projects. Often, when they actually list the costs and resources required they find the goal wasn't realistic at all. It's great to know that before you start! And great to know what you're going to need to fully achieve a realistic persuasion goal.

Specificity is your key to setting realistic, achievable persuasion goals. When you know precisely what you want, it's much easier to achieve that goal. The great comedian Lily Tomlin said it wonder-

Developing Persuasion Goals

Persuasion Goal:

Measurable Action:

Time Limit/ Target Date:

Estimated Resources (If Applicable):

Estimated Cost (If Applicable):

Complete Goal Statement:

You have taken the first step towards achieving your persuasion goal.

fully: "I always wanted to be somebody, but I should have been more specific."

When you have your specific goal elements determined, put them on paper or into your computer. Keep them visible. Constantly review and revise as necessary, but in written form. Don't let your brain fudge unwritten goals by saying, "Well, I didn't really mean that," and then excuse the measurement. Written goals are more motivating.

And of course when you have your goals set in specific, measurable terms, it will be much easier to translate those goals to the person you're persuading to act on those goals. When you persuade your partner to act, when you get compliance, he'll know exactly what he has agreed to. He can then more effectively structure the strategic and tactical steps to execute the goal.

The importance of setting measurable goals for your persuasion projects cannot be overstated. Goals are the starting point for all human achievement. Put your persuasion goals into an easy-to-communicate, easy-to-measure format and you'll be a lot closer to goal fulfillment.

REVIEW AND REFERENCE

- Knowing precisely what you want helps you achieve it. Success is determined by setting specific goals and then persuading others to execute and reach those goals.
- A well-stated, achievable goal must have four elements.
  1. A specific measurable action.
  2. A time limit or target date.
  3. A cost estimate, stated in dollars, energy, or effort.
  4. Identified resources, people, and/or material.
- The most important criterion is having a measurable standard. It is imperative that you have a clear goal to measure results against.

- Avoid the "someday" syndrome by setting specific time frames for decisions and actions.
- Set goals for costs and resources. Specificity is your key to setting realistic, achievable persuasion goals.
- When you have your specific goal elements determined, put them on paper or into your computer. Constantly review and revise as necessary, but in written form.
- When you have your goals set in specific, measurable terms, it will be much easier to translate those goals to the person you're persuading to act on those goals.
- For your CPO, current persuasion opportunity, we have an interactive form to help determine the most persuasive elements for your current persuasion goals. Go to www.seventriggers.com where you can select the applicable elements, make notes, and print them out.

Chapter 16

Persuasive Communication

A s leaders we often take communication for granted. We've been communicating for a lifetime and we consider it a simple, straightforward process. We know what we want to communicate, we tell people what's on our minds, and we're done. Unfortunately, true communication isn't that easy. Actually, successful communication is rather complex. And yes, it's difficult. And the difficulty of achieving full understanding is exacerbated by the fact that most people do not understand the difference between talking, telling, and communicating.

I know you already know how to communicate, but hang with me on this. Effective, persuasive communication is far different from the day-to-day version. The form, content, and delivery of your communication will determine your persuasion success or failure.

Successful, result-oriented communication takes knowledge, thought, planning, and execution. As Harvard Business School professor Michael Hattersley put it, "All business communication aims to achieve a result. When successful, it moves its audience to do something—to buy a product, change behavior, support a plan or adopt a point of view." Our goal is to communicate in a way that moves our partner to do something. To produce the result you seek. And that takes a skilled approach.

When communication is not effective, when it is not successful, confusion reigns. "What do you mean it's wrong?" "But I thought you said . . ." "Yes, I heard you, but I thought you meant . . ."

Persuasion success depends entirely on communication. Successful persuasion is communication. But of course if it's not clear, it's not communication. Let's see if we can determine how to create the results we seek with effective communication.

WHAT THEY HEAR IS WHAT THEY GET

Communication—we use it all day, every day. How would you describe communication? Please stop for a minute to consider your own definition.

We watch TV for untold hours—does the TV communicate? When people are arguing, are they communicating? In any discussion, who determines what is being communicated?

Webster's New Collegiate Dictionary offers the following definition: "A process by which information is exchanged between individuals through a common system of symbols or behavior." Not bad, as far as it goes; yet it says little about what is actually communicated, and by whom. It says nothing about the intended understandings versus the perceptions of what was communicated. The definition does, however, eliminate what many consider communication by requiring that "information is exchanged."

Our definition of communication goes to the heart of communicating for a purpose.

"True communication is not what the sender intends to communicate; it is what the receiver understands."

This is a very important concept, and somewhat difficult to fully appreciate. I know what I want to communicate and I know what I think I did communicate, but you may well perceive something entirely different from what I meant. So here's the kicker: whatever your partner thinks he heard and what he thinks you meant, that's what was communicated. What you intended has little relevancy to the real world of communication.

189

There are an infinite number of causes for differences in what was intended, how it was interpreted, and what is perceived. Reasons for these discrepancies are a subject for a full book. The reality is, this potential difference in interpretation is an issue we have to address and avoid. Please remember this: the message we think we communicated is very seldom the message the other person perceives he heard.

How then do you determine what the other person perceives he or she heard? You must get feedback! You must question your partner to determine what her perception is. This is a bit tricky. Ask the wrong way, and you'll insult your partner. "Of course I understand you!" The better approach is to ask for her opinion regarding the issue. Then ask how she might proceed to the goal.

Ask a question that will reveal the perception, but that will not belittle the partner.

Rather than asking, "Have I made myself clear?" Try, "Charlie, how would you see this change initiative unfolding?" Or, "What do you see as the next steps?"

Communicating for results is a four-step process.

1. Organize your content into a presentation framework.
2. Deliver the information.
3. Check for perceptions—get feedback.
4. Agree on action steps.

Only when you have feedback will you know if your communication was interpreted the way you intended. Only when you know what was actually communicated can you proceed to the action steps.

This brings up the next item. Whose responsibility is it to ascertain that the communication is received as intended? The answer: you, the sender, have the prime responsibility; though both parties must actively participate and share in the process.

The process as we have described it is essential to effective communication, essential to a meeting of the minds, essential to achieving a result. Communicating to persuade, communicating for a purpose is an involved, interactive process that requires strong questioning and listening skills. Unfortunately, most of us vastly overrate our communication skills. And we wonder why "he just doesn't get it"!

True communication occurs only when the message is received and understood as intended.

TELLING OR COMMUNICATING?

Does the TV set communicate? Not by our definition. The TV only gives out information. Giving out information is hardly communication. It doesn't even meet the dictionary definition of communication, "information is exchanged." TV is not interactive. There is no exchange of information. Yet don't we often act just like the TV— don't we frequently merely give out information and think we're communicating? Effective communication is interactive, and interactive communication allows us to connect with our partner. Telling is one-way information dissemination, but telling is not communicating.

When we engage in one-way communication, when we tell people what we want done, we often have no idea what was actually communicated. The partner may perceive that you're just being heavy-handed, unreasonable, off the wall, or simply taking a wrong tack. He may perceive something entirely different from what you intended.

ASK, LISTEN, UNDERSTAND

Our goal is to create communication in which you understand the other person and she in turn understands you. Persuasion works best when partners truly understand each other.

Effective communication is dependent on our knowledge and application of two key skills: questioning and listening. If we are weak in either area, we risk poor, inaccurate communication that will not motivate people to comply. With good questioning and listening skills, you can build a strong partnership to achieve mutual goals.

LEARN ABOUT YOUR PARTNER

Your first communication and persuasion goal is to learn as much as possible about your partner. The more you learn, the better you will know how to frame your proposal. What are his thoughts regarding the issue at hand and what internal triggers will propel him in the direction you want? What are his past actions in similar situations? What are his preconceived ideas? Is he likely to act in the heavy analytical thinking mode or in the automatic mode? What values will he reinforce? What criteria will influence his decisions and actions?

QUESTIONS ARE THE ANSWER

To become a persuasive communicator, questions are the answer. Questions are crucial to persuasion, and the right question at the right time makes the difference between success and failure. In fact, the use of questions may make the difference between success and failure in our lives.

A cover article in the *New York Times Magazine* presented research indicating that happiness itself is based on our skill and application of questions. The research showed that the happiest people were active questioners. The most unhappy and loneliest people were those who asked few questions of others.

Questions create interactivity which in turn creates understanding and positive relationships. The goal of persuasive communications is not to inform our partner about ourselves, it is to inform ourselves about our partner.

"The only way to influence the other fellow," Dale Carnegie suggested, "is to talk about what he wants and show him how to get it." How do we learn what the other fellow wants? The nineteenth-century British Prime Minister Benjamin Disraeli provides the answer, "The fool wonders, the wise man asks."

The wise man also periodically reinforces what he already knows. The following is basic stuff, Communications 101, and you already know it. But hang in there—a review won't hurt, and chances are you will pick up a detail or two you forgot or aren't using as effectively as possible. Getting the information we need is pivotal to successful persuasion. Author Rudyard Kipling provides a clue to how we obtain it.

> I keep six honest serving-men
> (They taught me all I knew);
> Their names are What and Why and When
> And How and Where and Who

How we employ these six honest serving men, the order and placement of these questions, is essential to getting the persuasion results we seek. The right question at the right time will make you a powerful and successful communicator.

Let's break the six honest men into two categories, each with a specific goal. The categories are

- Open-ended questions
- Closed-ended questions

Open-ended questions are used to get your partner talking—to get him to open up and share the general information you seek. These questions are:

- What?
- Why?
- How?

They cannot usually be answered with a word or two—they require a longer, more general answer.

Closed-ended questions are employed to obtain very specific information and answers. They include:

- When?
- Where?
- Who?

These questions elicit a simple, often one-word answer.

To get your partner to open up, you might ask, "What are your goals regarding these departmental changes we are proposing?"

To learn specifics, you might use a closed-ended question, "If we go forward, who in your department could manage this project?" The answer will likely be one word.

The learning step here is to know when to use each type of question.

Open-ended questions are best employed early in the conversation. Well structured, they will elicit volumes of information. Open questions are also used to get your partner to elaborate on a topic, to give you more information. Questions like: "How do you see this unfolding?" or "Why would you take that approach?" will provide insights you need to persuade. Open questions are also an excellent way to get your partner talking if the conversation lags.

Closed questions are employed after you have developed an overall, general picture of the landscape. They prompt specific answers to specific issues not covered in the general conversation. And very importantly, closed questions allow you to steer the conversation in your direction. Open questions allow the partner to go off on tangents, whereas closed questions bring him back to the subject. Example: "Charlie, that's a great fishing story, love to go there with you—but let me ask, when do you think we could begin work on this change program?"

TO PERSUADE, LEARN VALUES

To effectively actuate your partner's internal triggers, you must learn a bit about those triggers. For example, with the hope and consistency triggers you must know what he will be consistent with and what he hopes to accomplish. You need to learn what he values, and the order of relative importance of the potential criteria he'll consider.

We get the answers through a questioning process called value profiling. The answers will tell you what he will be consistent with, what he hopes to achieve, and will provide clues to determine if he is in the analytical or automatic thinking mode.

There are two types of value profiling, formal and informal.

In the formal mode, you prepare a list of relevant questions, starting with a general open-ended question. You then list several pertinent questions or issues, and ask your partner to rate the value of each as a one, a two, or a three. The ones are very important, a two somewhat important, and a three—forget about it.

I know applying this system sounds a bit cumbersome, but you will be amazed at how easy it is to use and you'll delight in the excellent information you receive. You'll not only learn what your partner values, you'll learn a critical bit of knowledge—the relative importance of these values.

The informal value profile consists of a series of open-ended questions, hopefully prepared before the presentation. These might include questions like, "For this departmental reorganization, what do you see as the critical issues?" or, "What concerns do you have about the changes we propose?" At the end of an informal value profile, you might clarify any issues with closed questions. You might then ask, "You've mentioned several criteria of interest to you, how would you rank these in order of importance?" Answers to these questions are magic for the skilled persuader. Your partner will not only tell you how to activate her internal triggers, she'll tell you in what order to present information for the most compelling effect.

In the previously cited book *The Cardinal Rules of Advocacy*, author Levine calls his most important rule "cardinal rule number one": "The necessity of properly identifying your audience and tailoring your arguments to its needs." You can only tailor your arguments to the correct needs when you have diligently probed to understand them. Believing you already know your partner's wants and needs is fraught with danger. Get it right—ask.

Put simply, value profiling is persuasion's quintessential application of open and closed questions. The answers give you incredible leverage in gaining the compliance you seek. They tell you precisely how to frame, tailor, then execute your presentation.

THE OTHER HALF OF COMMUNICATION

Now we deal with the other half of communication. You've asked the right questions, but how well do you listen to the answers? Consider the following questions.

- Do you just hear the words, or do you actively search for the hidden meanings?
- Do you fully absorb the meanings so you can deal with them in your presentation?
- Are you actively listening, or are you thinking about what to say next?
- Is active listening really that important to your leadership persuasion success?

Dean Rusk, JFK's secretary of state put listening in perspective: "One of the best ways to persuade others is with your ears—by listening to them."

Active Listening Diagram

SPEAKER

ENCODES MESSAGE
*"My son has just been
awarded a football
scholarship!"*

PASSIVE LISTENER
"That's nice...Zzz"

RESPONSE
"Conversation dies"

ACTIVE LISTENER

**VERBAL MESSAGE
RECEIVED**
• *Words*

**NONVERBAL
MESSAGE
READ**
• *Facial expression*
• *Use of hands*
• *Enthusiasm*
• *Pride*

RESPONSE
*"You must have helped
your son do well in school.
Congratulations! You must
be proud!"*

ENCOURAGES MORE INFO!

Passive listening is easy. Active listening requires attention and thought.

Example: A woman you know tells you her son just got a full tuition football scholarship to the University of Notre Dame. The passive, poor listener might comment, "Gee, that's terrific!" and the conversation would be over.

What would the active listener do? What encoded message is she delivering?

The active listener might say, "Wow! You must be really proud of your son—how did you help him get such good grades to even be considered by such a great college?" He's connected with the other party—communication is interactive. It's working. Your challenge is to decode all the coded messages you get—and keep the conversation interactive. Active listening is hard work, but the payoff is worth the extra effort.

MIRRORING

The final element we'll cover in our review of persuasive communications is called mirroring. In the friendship trigger we shared information about the innate trigger that is activated when people perceive us to be like them. The closer we are to their views, background, shared values, and actions, the easier it is to employ the friendship trigger. Looking and acting similarly to our partner communicates a strong sense of friendship.

Our ability to mirror the other person's tone, voice, cadence, and enthusiasm, to match his dress and mannerisms, all play a significant role in our ability to communicate persuasively. If he's laid back and easygoing, be the same. If he's quick and to the point, you'll turn him off with slow, easygoing, pedantic communication. Match his tone of voice, rate of speech, and gestures. We trust and befriend those we perceive to be like us.

We're not recommending monkey see, monkey do, but we strongly suggest you follow your partner's lead. When you mirror your partner, you trigger strong automatic positive reactions.

And finally, pay close attention to your nonverbal actions. Studies conducted by Dr. Albert Mehrabian at the University of Southern California indicate that a surprising amount of total information is communicated not by the words we use, but by the actions that accompany those words.

Mehrabian documented that only 7 percent of total communication is determined by the words we use. More important than the words was the way we said the words—38 percent of what was perceived stems from *how* we say the words. But here's the real surprise—the balance of the 100 percent of what was actually communicated emanated from the non-verbal signals given. If you've done the math, you've figured out that 55 percent of what we communicate is determined by our non-verbal actions.

What we say is important. How we say it, how we match our intonations to the words is more important. Our nonverbal cues are critical. Pay attention to each communication element to successfully communicate for compliance.

The web, email, cell phones, pagers, VoIP technology all help us communicate more easily, but not necessarily more effectively. The true goal of communication, particularly persuasive communication, is to understand and to be understood. That's hard work. To persuade, to gain willing compliance, you must communicate to understand, not just to inform or educate.

Amateurs give out information. Partners use interactive communication to emotionally connect with the other person. The communication skills provided here will enable you to connect with your partner to achieve mutually beneficial persuasion goals.

Listening Dos and Don'ts

Don'ts	Dos
Think of what to say next.	Actively listen.
Interrupt the speaker.	Seek connections between ideas.
Let your attention stray.	Listen for main ideas.
Respond superficially.	Interpret encoded message.
Fail to concentrate.	Concentrate on what is being said and why.
Control by talking.	Control by listening then questioning.
Ignore nonverbal messages.	Watch nonverbal clues.
Evaluate your point of view.	Evaluate speaker's point of view.
React before understanding.	React after understanding.
Argue, respond emotionally.	Stifle emotional reaction.
Ignore tone and emotions.	Be aware of tone and emotions.
Document everything.	Take brief notes.
Put the speaker down.	Empathize.
Frown.	Smile.
Talk too much.	Use silence to get information.

REVIEW AND REFERENCE

- All persuasion communication hopes to move our partner to do something. Yet the message we think we communicate is very seldom the message our partner perceives.
- Communicating for results is a four-step process.
  1. Organize your content into a presentation framework.
  2. Deliver the information.
  3. Check for perceptions—get feedback.
  4. Agree on action steps.
- Effective communication is dependent on two key skills: questioning and listening.
- Open-ended questions are best employed early in the conversation. They get your partner talking—to open up and share the general information you seek. These questions are what, why, and how. They cannot usually be answered with a word or two—they require a longer, more general answer.
- Closed-ended questions are employed to obtain specific information and answers. They include when, where, and who. These questions elicit a simple, often one-word answer. Closed questions allow you to steer the conversation in your direction.
- Value profiling uncovers partner values and decision-making criteria. The value profile tells you precisely how to frame, tailor, then execute your presentation.
  - Active listening requires attention and thought.
  - Don't just hear the answers; actively search for the encoded hidden meanings.
  - Fully absorb the meanings so you can deal with them in your presentation.
  - Actively listen, don't just think about what to say next.
- Looking and acting similar to our partner communicates a strong sense of friendship.

201

- When you mirror your partner's tone, mannerisms, and dress you trigger automatic positive reactions.
- Be aware of your nonverbal actions, because they determine 55 percent of what we communicate. The way we say the words is far more important than the words we say.
- For your CPO, current persuasion opportunity, we have an interactive form to help determine the most persuasive elements for your immediate persuasion challenge. Go to www.seventriggers .com where you can select the applicable elements, make notes, print them out.

Chapter 17

Persuasive
Presentations

ow the rubber meets the road. What will you do with all of this persuasion knowledge? How will you most effectively execute your persuasion process? What will you do and say to maximize your chances for getting full, willing compliance from your partner? Right—you will communicate your wishes to your partner. You'll present your proposal.

To some, the connotation of "proposal" sounds like a sales pitch. In reality, virtually everything we communicate to others is a proposal of sorts. CEO coach Tony Jeary authored a best seller titled *Life Is a Series of Presentations.* Jeary states, "[C]all them presentation skills or people skills, these practices will allow you to master any interaction, whether it involves a roomful of colleagues, a small group, or just one other person. . . . The way in which we present our thoughts and ideas to people, from our colleagues at work to our spouse and even the person waiting on us at the grocery store could have a profound effect on the shape of our own lives."

Jeary defines a presentation as what you are trying to communicate at the moment. We'll therefore call the formulation, framing, and execution of your persuasion content your presentation. How well you plan, then execute, the presentation will determine your success or failure.

In *Mozart's Brain and the Fighter Pilot,* Dr. Restak gives us the best possible advice for framing our presentation: "Apply your knowledge about the human brain to organize your thoughts."

As we have said so many times, we want to work with our partner's natural brain processes rather than forcing the brain to act in unnatural ways.

You now realize that we make most decisions based on the amygdala's initial emotional response. If we deal with rationality and logic at all, it is to reinforce those decisions with information later sent to the prefrontal cortex. A properly framed presentation will be more easily understood and acted upon by the amygdala.

The organization, structure, framing, and flow of your proposal are absolutely critical for reaching your persuasion goal. The way you deliver that well-framed presentation is equally important.

Ancient Rome's great persuader Cicero had the following to say on presentation organization: "However beautiful and alluring his words may be, if he just pours them out in a meaningless flow, he will be behaving like a fool."

Lyle Sussman, professor of management at the University of Louisville puts organization in perspective, in his article for *Business Horizons* called "How to Frame a Message: The Art of Persuasion and Negotiation." "Persuasive content needs a focused context," he says. "Framing gives perspective, rationale, and structure to what you need to say."

Now, I know you would never propose anything in a meaningless flow of words and information. But unfortunately, most people do not plan and execute a strong, well-framed, meaningful flow of information. That flow must present information in a framework your partner can easily, automatically understand. If there's no understanding, there's no true communication, and no persuasion. I have witnessed thousands of presentations, and precious few are well organized and executed. The result is predictable. Too few persuade as effectively as they should.

GREAT ARGUMENTS DO NOT PERSUADE

Writing in *Harvard Business Review,* Dr. Jay Conger lists four key ways *not* to persuade; ways that make persuasion difficult, if not impossible. One of Conger's top four persuasion inhibitors is "Thinking that the secret of persuasion lies in presenting great arguments."

Conger and persuasion cognoscenti recognize, as I hope you now realize, that great arguments do not persuade.

This documented finding is our breakthrough. It is a cataclysmic, fundamental departure from what most of us believed before in vivo brain imaging documented the brain's real-time information processing.

I recognize that this new information, like other great truths, will take time to accept. It will meet with skepticism. Yet we now know unequivocally that well-framed presentations focused on the amygdala's internal triggers persuade and gain compliance faster and more effectively than great arguments, data, reason, and logic.

Remember the total, powerful restructuring of the giant GE corporation? Jack Welch didn't persuade people to accomplish this gargantuan task with great arguments, with reason and logic. No, he employed two simple triggers in a few sentences. "Fixed, sold, or closed" went right to the amygdala. Welch persuaded. He gained compliance. He succeeded.

One of the biggest contributors to persuasion failure is to offer points or arguments that are compelling to us, believing they will be compelling to others. That's a poor assumption and it doesn't work. Thanks to the new discoveries in neuroscience we can finally, knowingly work in concert with the brain's natural processes rather than work against them. And to work in sync with the brain, we have to frame the presentation to meet the brain's natural flow.

Conger adds, "There is as much strategy in how you present your position as in the position itself. In fact, I'd say the strategy of the presentation is the more critical." We're going to share the strategy, and the tactics to execute that strategy.

What do we mean by a "presentation"? Reprising Professor Hattersley's comment, "All business communication aims to achieve a result," you are communicating, presenting, all day, every day, to virtually everyone. Your presentation can be informal, a seemingly ad hoc discussion at your desk over a cup of coffee. It can be a "chance" meeting at any location, in the car, at the club, at your kitchen table. It can be an appointment at a convenient venue.

The presentation can be highly formal—a meeting to explore specific issues with pertinent personnel at a specific pre-scheduled time and location. You may have a wealth of audiovisual and print material to share. But, a presentation can be any and all communications with others. For our purpose, a presentation is the process of communicating your persuasion message to those who will execute the results you seek.

How then do we frame our presentation for utmost impact, for the best chance to gain the right decision, to get full compliance? Let's start with some preliminaries.

These preliminaries require us to package, to organize all the persuasion elements into a plan, a framework for your message.

The first step is so obvious it's often missed. It's missed because we take it for granted that we know what we want. Truth is, in most cases we do not know what we want in finite detail. The first step is to know precisely, in definitive terms, your persuasion goal. Exactly what do you want your partner to do in compliance with your request? Of course you have an overall idea—but is your goal reduced to writing? Are at least two elements of the four-step goal process, a measurable standard and a time frame, well documented?

As a first step, write down exactly what you hope to accomplish, and precisely what you expect your partner to do as the first step in commitment. Then jot down your time frame—when you'll make your proposal, when it should be acted upon, and when it should be completed.

Second, list the questions you will ask your partner to determine his perceptions on the issue at hand. This will be your value profile, formal or informal. With these questions you will be able to learn the information you need to make an informed presentation.

BRAINSTORM THE TRIGGERS

Now comes the make-or-break, pivotal part of your planning process. How well you do this third part will determine your end result. Grab a yellow pad, the back of an envelope, a napkin, or open an MS Word document. List, one by one, each of the seven internal triggers. Then refer back to each trigger chapter, to the Trigger Elements, the lists of potential issues for each of the seven triggers. For each trigger, jot down any and all elements that might activate your partner's internal triggers. Under each trigger, creatively list every possible item that could conceivably apply to your partner.

You will find an interactive form to easily accomplish your trigger analysis and planning on our Web site—www.seventriggers.com.

As you create your list, use the brainstorming technique—first get the items down with no qualitative evaluation. Qualify later.

Do the same with each trigger, listing all of the possible applications for each. You might even add your own triggers.

Will each trigger have equal value in every presentation? Of course not. Yet until you get all of your creative information down in writing, you will not know which internal trigger might best activate the response you seek. For some triggers you'll generate a long list of items, for others, a shorter list. Get them all down before taking the next step.

Now go back over each list and highlight the most realistic, most applicable items for each trigger.

Next, determine from your lists which triggers will provide the most impact for the specific partner and issue under consideration, those that are most likely to impact your partner's emotions. And, of course, determine which triggers offer the best content for your meeting. Each situation determines how many triggers and which triggers to select for that issue. I usually select the four or five triggers most applicable to the current situation. I'll use them in the presentation, keeping the others in reserve.

Finally, prioritize your trigger list to determine in which order you will present the trigger information.

While this preliminary phase can be done as suggested on a yellow pad or an envelope, I find that the easiest, most effective way to organize trigger information is in Microsoft Word. I use the "outline mode" in Word since it's easy to create the outline, then to move things around as you prioritize, change, and delete. Better yet, work with the interactive form on the seventriggers.com Web site.

You are now ready to organize, to frame your delivery. Here's the typical framework most of us use, and one I've seen a thousand times.

- State your position—put sufficient emphasis and strength into your thoughts and ideas.
- Present your supporting information, with reason, logic, and data.
- Make your points and get agreement.
- Emphasize the logic and reason for your arguments; use persistence and your own enthusiasm to wrap up the commitment.

To again quote Jay Conger's article in *Harvard Business Review*, "Following this process is one sure fire way to fail at persuasion." This four-step process is the time-honored approach most of us use. It is therefore difficult to appreciate that it is very inefficient, a sure fire way to fail. There is a better way.

Trigger Application Worksheet

For each Trigger, list all elements that will potentially activate that trigger. Refer to Trigger Elements list in each trigger chapter.

Friendship Trigger

Authority Trigger

Consistency Trigger

Reciprocity Trigger

Contrast Trigger

Reason Why Trigger

Hope Trigger

Harvard Business School Professor Nitin Nohria comments on the documentation we try to bring into our proposals: "In addition to minimizing resistance, avoiding the use of numbers and other hard data helps managers avoid the cognitive limitations of the human mind."

How then do we frame a successful proposal, one that will appeal to the emotions, and avoid the cognitive limitations of the human mind? Put simply, your presentation must be as basic, as easy to understand as possible. It must fit your personality and style, and still be focused on your partner.

The actual format, the framing of the presentation, will vary depending on how formal or informal the presentation will be. The framing will depend on your partner, and the issue under consideration. Within those variables, it's up to you to create the frame and then fill it in.

Every presentation is analogous to a speech or a written article. It has a beginning, a body, and a wrap. The body will employ much of the trigger information and will be structured accordingly. It is critical to structure the framework of your presentation, and at the same time keep it interactive and flexible. After all, the presentation is designed for your partner to interact with you; it must not be your monologue. Your partner may want to go off on tangents—that's fine, go with him, let him roam! Your structured framework allows you to get back on target after each tangent.

Frame your presentation so that the beginning and the ending have the highest impact and are the most memorable. The friendship trigger, perhaps accompanied by the reciprocity trigger, is always a great start. Establish the friendship elements, and all else flows better. Refer back to the friendship trigger unit for "how to" information.

Unless your partner is already aware of your credibility in the specific area of discussion, you will want early application of the authority trigger. In a nonboastful way, establish your credentials, your knowledge, credibility, research, and expertise.

Your value profile, the answers to your questions, are critical in determining how you will conduct the rest of the conversation. So plan to ask these questions up front.

Framing the body of the presentation is easy. Refer to the top triggers you selected, and establish the priority order for presenting each bit of information for each trigger.

If, for example, the conformity trigger is important to your partner, prepare a list of all the people, companies, or entities that are benefiting from what you propose. As noted in the conformity section we do this by showing a list of all the companies that have purchased a specific training program, and then we show documentation of the results they have achieved.

The hope trigger is always in play for everyone. Your frame should include a list of questions whose answers will tell you precisely what your partner hopes for in the current situation.

The "guts" of your proposal, including the logic and data, will follow the trigger information. Logic and data will reinforce the positive decision you will have generated. Logic and data must be used as reinforcement, not to generate the decision or action you seek. Remember that when you ask your partner to evaluate the hard data areas, you're asking him to put his hands into ice water, to endure pain, to deal with 300 percent more effort. Do the hard lifting with planning and research so he doesn't have to.

Finally, frame your wrap. Use your goal documentation to list what you want your partner to do—the specific decisions and actions you seek. Then determine how you will request this action.

Here's a basic frame sample:

- Goal
- Introduction
- Reciprocity trigger

- Friendship trigger
- Authority trigger
- Value profile
- Body
  - Hope trigger
  - Conformity trigger
  - Back-up data
- Resolve resistance
- Get commitment
- Documentation/leave-behind material
- Wrap

Within this outline you will fill in all the points, all the information you will present to emotionally involve the amygdala to gain quick, automatic commitment and to finalize agreement. The better your plan, the better your framing, the more productive your execution will be.

INTO THE FOOTLIGHTS

Now comes the fun part, your time in the footlights, communicating your hard work to your partner. How do you most effectively set the stage and execute the delivery?

Your first and very significant consideration is the venue. Where is the best place to communicate your proposal and goal? Everyone knows about the home court advantage. Where possible, use it! If at all possible, conduct your discussion on your turf. Get a meeting in your office, your own home, any venue that provides the home turf advantage.

Second best venue is neutral turf. A restaurant, ballpark, or golf course. The cafeteria, lounge, or meeting room. If using a neutral venue, say a restaurant, make the turf "yours" by selecting the restaurant, and by picking up the tab.

Worst case—the other person's turf. Avoid it or lose the home turf advantage.

Turf selection is more critical to persuasion than most realize. You are communicating for a goal—give yourself every opportunity to achieve that goal.

How will you physically interact with your partner? Sitting across a desk or table is OK, but not great. There is a physical and psychological barrier between you. And unless you are good at reading upside down, you cannot easily share written or graphic information. Sitting next to each other is better—but it's hard to maintain crucial eye contact. Best bet is to sit at a forty-five-degree angle with your partner. You can share written information, common space, and maintain eye contact.

How about the physical material you've prepared and plan to use? If you have items you want your partner to look at, to go through, when and how should you provide them? There is a hard-and-fast rule here. Never give your partner material until you are ready to go over it with her. And then, only the specific piece you want to share and discuss.

Why not give it to her at the outset? You stand the possibility, the probability of losing control, of losing concentration. She may look through the material and not pay attention to your conversation. She'll go to where she wants in the material, not where you want. Losing control with back-up material is a risk you don't want to take.

If you have leave-behind material, give it to her when you leave—not before.

Now you have framework and the setup. Make your conversation highly interactive. Maintain interest and enthusiasm by asking questions, sharing opinions, doing anything to keep your partner involved.

Stay on the track set by your framing, but let your partner dictate the side roads. Return to your frame to get back on the main road.

Sample Presentation Framework

Goal

Introduction

Friendship Trigger

Reciprocity Trigger

Introduce Persuasion Topic

Authority Trigger

Value Profile Questions

Body

Hope Trigger

Conformity Trigger

Back Up Data

Resolve Resistance, Anticipated Issues

Get Commitment-Closure

Wrap, Confirm Next Steps

Apply the value profile to learn not only what your partner values, but to determine her current thinking mode, analytical or automatic. If you are dealing with an analytic, a lawyer, accountant, or IT person for example, you may want to go a little heavier on the logic and reason. Remember however that most people all the time and all people most of the time are in the automatic mode.

Planning your conversation and discussion points in advance, and then executing those points as planned will go a long way to achieving the decisions and actions you want.

When your thoughts are well organized, you have a much better chance to help your partner fully understand what you want and why. Any confusion, any lack of understanding results in nondecisions. Good framing, clarity, and brevity in execution lead to understanding and acceptance.

We know persuasion is a process, not an event. Sometimes you need to persuade on the spot, say during an incoming phone call, or when making a quick response to an email. Process may not be an option. How can you activate the right triggers? I keep lists of the seven triggers attached to my computer, to my phone, and in my wallet. I scan them as the communication flows, and activate any triggers that will help. As you create the habit of providing the right information to engage specific internal triggers, you'll find the results amazing.

Even if your partner is an Einstein, he will benefit from emotion and imagination. Einstein said, "When I examine myself and my methods of thought, I come to the conclusion that the gift of fantasy has meant more to me than my talent for absorbing positive knowledge."

Use the "positive knowledge" sparingly, sow the emotional seeds of fantasy, all the good feelings, the values, the realized hopes that will be earned when he commits to your proposal.

G. Michael Campbell, author of *Bulletproof Presentations*, states, "Facts alone will not influence someone else's thoughts, actions or feelings. Appealing to emotions will make a presentation memorable."

Frame, then execute your presentation to be easily understood. Use internal emotion triggers to make your presentation memorable. Do these things and you will succeed in your persuasion goal.

REVIEW AND REFERENCE

- Presentation describes any communication with those you wish to persuade.
- A presentation can take any degree of formality ranging from an ad hoc discussion at your home or desk to a scheduled meeting.
- The first step to framing a presentation is to know, in definitive terms, your persuasion goal—and reduce it to writing. This goal should include what you hope to accomplish, what you expect your partner to do, and the time frame.
- Second, list the questions you will ask your partner to determine his perceptions on the issue at hand. This will be your value profile, formal or informal.
- List each of the seven internal triggers, and under each one, list every possible item that could apply to your partner. Next, highlight the most realistic, most applicable items for each trigger. Select three or four triggers best suited to the specific situation. Then prioritize your trigger list to determine in which order you will present the trigger information.
- Frame your presentation with the beginning and the ending having the highest impact. The friendship trigger coupled with the reciprocity trigger is a great start. You will also want early application of the authority trigger.
- The "guts" of your proposal, including the logic and data, will follow the trigger information. Minimal application of logic and data will reinforce the positive decision.

- Finally, frame your closure. Define precisely what you want your partner to do—the specific decisions and actions you seek. Then determine how you will request this action.
- Here's a basic frame sample:
  - Goal
  - Introduction
  - Reciprocity trigger
  - Friendship trigger
  - Authority trigger
  - Value profile
  - Body
    - Hope trigger
    - Conformity trigger
    - Back-up data
- Resolution of resistance
- Getting a commitment
- Documentation/leave-behind material
- Wrap
- For your CPO, current persuasion opportunity, we have an interactive form to help determine the most persuasive elements for your presentation. Go to www.seventriggers.com where you can select the applicable elements, make notes, and print them out.

Chapter 18

Resolving Resistance

oes your partner always fully agree with everything you say during a presentation? Is there often some resistance? If there is disagreement on points or issues, if there are questions, even objections to your comments, how are these stated? And most important, how do you react and respond?

Most people hate resistance. They get flustered, go off target, grow defensive, even become argumentative. Many view resistance or objections as negative elements of the persuasive communication process. Many, faced with resistance, back away from their persuasion efforts. Learn the right responses and you'll actually welcome resistance. Resistance and objections are an inevitable part of the persuasion process, and the good news is that we can learn to enjoy and profit from resistance and objections.

How can objections be a positive element in our persuasion attempt? When you get an objection to a statement or idea, if your partner questions something you said, what is the probable encoded message he's sending? In all likelihood, he's saying, "I need more information." Is this a good thing or bad? It's great! Why? Because it shows interest, involvement. Because it tells you precisely what you have to do to quell the resistance.

Questions may seem like resistance, but they are your keys to knowing how to proceed. "Rejoice when the court asks questions. And again I say rejoice!" John W. Davis proclaimed in a speech to lawyers of the New York Bar Association. "If the question does nothing more, it gives you the assurance that the court is not comatose and that you have awakened at least a vestigial interest."

I hope you will rejoice at resistance and objections. They show life, interest, involvement, and tell you exactly where you missed a step or two. They tell you they're interested, and inform you regarding what questions must be answered.

The secret to loving objections is to know how to react to them, and how to resolve the resistance. How do most people react to resistance? Here are typical responses:

- We push back at resistance with a somewhat forceful response— sometimes even argue.
- We react emotionally. We get upset.
- We get defensive.
- Sometimes we ignore resistance.
- We lose concentration and direction.
- We act condescendingly, sometimes even use ridicule.
- We lose confidence in ourselves and our proposal.

These responses are counterproductive; they will not help us persuade. The wrong response to objections can throw the entire persuasion process off track.

GOLDEN OPPORTUNITIES

Before sharing the best responses to resistance, let's define resistance as a potential roadblock to what you're trying to accomplish. Complaints and gripes are not objections. These are things you may have to listen to, but they probably have little direct impact on the issue at hand. We're classifying an objection as a specifically voiced deterrent to obtaining agreement for the decision you seek. And we define an objection as a golden opportunity. Why? Because objections tell you what you need to resolve. Is it better to have potential questions out on the table where you can deal with them, or stuck as unknown negatives in your partner's head? Objections are requests for more information, and can therefore be easily addressed and eliminated.

One secret to successfully responding to objections is to know that all objections are not created equal. Some, like the smoke screen objection, are offered to disguise the real objection. "I'm satisfied with the way things are—no need to implement something new." What this really means is: "You haven't given me sufficient motivation to change my operations."

Stalls and put-offs are not sincere objections. "I really have to think about this for a while." Faced with a stall, probe to learn the real reason for "thinking about it." You might ask, "What specifically can I help you think about?" Conduct your questioning—open and closed—until you find the sincere objection. Once you learn what's really on his mind, the issue requiring more information, you're on your way to successfully filling in the missing pieces.

We employ a simple, four-step process for resolving resistance, for creating golden opportunities from seemingly negative objections.

1. Listen to the entire objection.
2. Acknowledge the objection in a positive manner.
3. Analyze the objection.
4. Answer the objection.

It's critical to allow your partner to get the objection fully out on the table where you can deal with it. Don't finish his sentence. Don't cut him off. Even ask, "Is there anything else?" You want all the information you can get.

Let the objection fall softly. Acknowledge it. Say, "I can understand why you feel that way." You may not agree with it, may not understand it at all; but he does feel that way, so you might as well soften the issue by acknowledging it.

Resolving Resistance

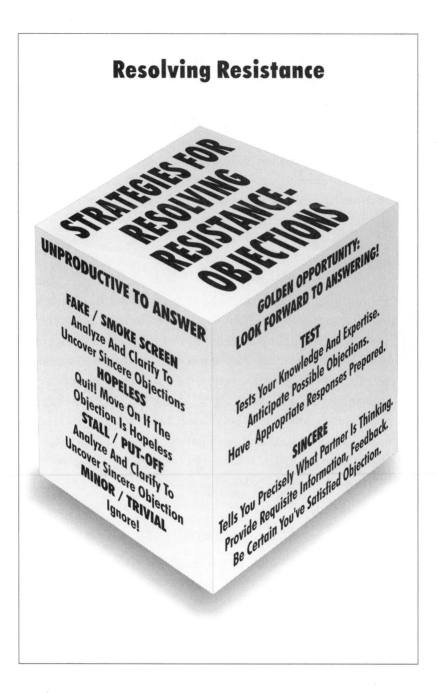

STRATEGIES FOR RESOLVING RESISTANCE: OBJECTIONS

UNPRODUCTIVE TO ANSWER

FAKE / SMOKE SCREEN
Analyze And Clarify To
Uncover Sincere Objections

HOPELESS
Quit! Move On If The
Objection Is Hopeless

STALL / PUT-OFF
Analyze And Clarify To
Uncover Sincere Objection

MINOR / TRIVIAL
Ignore!

**GOLDEN OPPORTUNITY:
LOOK FORWARD TO ANSWERING!**

TEST
Tests Your Knowledge And Expertise.
Anticipate Possible Objections.
Have Appropriate Responses Prepared.

SINCERE
Tells You Precisely What Partner Is Thinking.
Provide Requisite Information, Feedback.
Be Certain You've Satisfied Objection.

Analyze the objection. Be sure you understand the issue from his point of view. Never assume you fully know where he's coming from. Ask questions. Rephrase his questions and feed them back for clarification. Ask the right questions and your partner might well answer his own questions. Example: "How would you see the resolution to this situation?"

When you're certain you have found the real objection, provide your best answer. And that answer should contain elements that will positively trigger the desired reaction. Then add a final question: "Does this answer your concern?"

DON'T TAKE THE BAIT

One further note on objections. Most leaders rise to a challenge. We love to debate, and we enjoy a spirited argument. Too often we get baited into considering an objection as an invitation to argue— to show how smart we are, to reinforce our points, and worse, to put the other guy down. But even if you win that argument, you lose! No one wins an argument, so don't be tempted. Resolve resistance in a friendly, highly professional manner, and you're getting much closer to final commitment. With practice, you'll learn that objections are truly golden opportunities on the road to achieving your persuasion goal.

REVIEW AND REFERENCE

- Resistance and objections are an inevitable yet profitable part of the persuasion process. When you get an objection to a statement or idea, in all likelihood your partner is saying, "I need more information." He is showing interest and involvement.
- Questions may seem like resistance, but they are your keys to knowing how to proceed.

- All objections are not created equal. Some, like the smoke screen, the stall, and the put-off are used to disguise the real objection. Ask questions until you find the sincere objection.
- We employ a simple, four-step process for resolving resistance.
  1. Listen to the entire objection.
  2. Acknowledge the objection in a positive manner.
  3. Analyze the objection.
  4. Answer the objection.
- After listening to the objection, acknowledge it. Say, "I can understand why you feel that way." You may not agree or completely understand, but since he does feel that way, show you understand.
- Analyze the objection. Understand the issue from her point of view. Ask questions. Rephrase her questions and feed them back for clarification. Your partner might well answer her own issues.
- When you're certain you have found the real objection, provide your best answer. Then add a final question: "Does this answer your concern?"
- No one wins an argument, so don't be tempted. Resolve resistance in a friendly, highly professional manner, and you're getting much closer to final commitment.
- For your CPO, current persuasion opportunity, we have an interactive form to help determine the most persuasive elements for your current persuasion goals. Go to www.seventriggers.com where you can select the applicable elements, make notes, and print them out.

Chapter 19

Getting Commitment

You've done a great job of planning and executing your persuasion process. You've learned your partner's values and defined the criteria he'll employ to make a decision. You've determined which internal triggers will be most effective to facilitate the decision. You've made an outstanding presentation targeting the emotional issues that will trigger the action you seek. You've resolved resistance and are on the road to a decision, to full commitment. With excellent communication, you've generated understanding and good feelings all around. Is there anything left to do?

There is, but here's a shocker. Most people never take the next critical step, the step that determines success or failure. Until you have commitment, agreement, and closure, you may well have nothing to show for your efforts.

Several large research projects including one conducted by Zig Ziglar's company document that fully 63 percent of all persuasion presentations end without a request for specific action, for final agreement. That failure to request and finalize a decision is a waste of time, effort, energy, and resources.

When you fail to formalize the agreement, your planning, preparation, and presentation have been wasted. Oh, sure, you may have created a good relationship, and you probably shared some good information. You may have even educated your partner. But is that your goal? Is education your final persuasion criteria?

We're going to borrow an easily understood term from our

friends in sales and marketing and refer to this final, most critical step as "closure." Unless you get closure, specific agreement to proceed, until you trigger "Yes!" you haven't persuaded the decision and action you seek.

DEFINE YOUR NEXT MOVE

What is closure? Why is it an absolute necessity? Closure is simply wrapping up the persuasion process by:

- Getting agreement on a defined decision.
- Confirming, perhaps documenting, the agreement reached.
- Obtaining agreement for how to proceed on an idea, a project, a solution, or change initiative.
- Defining the next step.
- Agreeing on a time frame for action.

If the project you propose is a multi-step situation, closure may include:

- Agreeing to meet with additional interested parties.
- Arranging your own follow-up meeting.
- Documenting all the "next step" requirements.

The short definition of closure is this: facilitating a firm decision to proceed as proposed.

And this definition brings up a critical question. Who really closes the deal—you or your partner? While it's up to you to facilitate the close, only your partner can make the final decision to say "yes," to comply and act. Your task is to help your partner reach, then acknowledge the desired decision and action steps.

One more thought about the close before sharing "how to do it" information. In our training programs we begin the workshops with a question: "What skills do you hope to acquire in this session?" With salespeople, experienced pros and neophytes, whether from multinationals and Fortune 500 giants, or from tiny mom and pop entrepreneurial shops, the answer is always the same. Two-thirds of the hands go up requesting "better closing skills."

This shows a rather sad, fundamental misconception about the process of closure. The misconception is that the persuader closes the deal. The erroneous belief is that there are some special phrases, tricks, voodoo incantations, and techniques that will make you a better closer. Those who believe this simply do not understand the process for gaining final agreement, for triggering "Yes!" And perhaps this is why some salespeople are viewed so negatively.

What is the secret to understanding closure? It's this. The close is not a separate, distinct element in the persuasion process. The final closure decision is initiated when you first meet with your partner, when you begin to speak. Remember the lawyer's opening statement regarding impact on jury verdicts?

The close is determined by everything you communicate to your partner. It is dependent on your learning the value profile, on delivering your information in the best possible framework, on employing applicable triggers, and on resolving resistance. When you've done all of this well, the close will be an integral element in the presentation—an automatic, foregone conclusion. But facilitating that conclusion, that final "Yes! Let's get started!" commitment requires a bit of help from you.

How do we help our partner finalize that decision, the agreement to act? How do we avoid being among the 63 percent who end a presentation without asking for a conclusion?

We start by knowing our goal. Perhaps the biggest reason two-thirds of all presentations end without a request for action is that most would-be persuaders do not know specifically what they want to accomplish. The lack of a carefully defined written closing goal inhibits us from asking for specific decisions and actions. A fuzzy, amorphous goal is almost impossible to understand by either party. And it's just as difficult to ask for.

FLIP YOUR BUSINESS CARD

Broadway's Belasco Theater is named for producer and impresario David Belasco. Belasco puts focused goals in real-world context. When a playwright approached Belasco in hopes of getting his play produced, Belasco would hand the writer his business card. The writer was instructed to write a synopsis of the play on the back of the card. If he could not define the play's goal effectively, succinctly, on the back of a business card, Belasco would not consider taking on the play.

Can you condense your focus on precisely what you want done at the end of your presentation? Can you write your persuasion closure goal on the back of your business card? Good. Do it! Jot it down and stick the card in your pocket. Pull it out before you communicate your presentation, and check it again when you finish. When you fine-tune your goal it will be made clear in your presentation. It is much better to ask for specifics than to get general agreements that may be subject to future interpretation.

How, then, do we facilitate the final agreement—that final "Yes! Let's go!"?

The short answer is to simply ask for the decision, request the action you want.

The longer answer is to recognize that people need help, support, and reinforcement when they have to commit. This is where the subtleties of closure arise. The human brain reacts better to some motivators than others. At the point of final commitment, we want to help our partner avoid the pain and agony of analytical labor. We want to impact the amygdala, not the prefrontal cortex. We want to save him from ice water, from 300 percent additional cognitive effort.

Why are people on the fence at the time of closure? What is it that keeps them from saying, "Yes, I'm committed!" The number one reason we tarry on that final decision is fear. Fear of what might happen. Fear of what might not happen. Fear that there may be a better solution. Fear that the timing isn't right. Fear of what others may think.

When activated, our internal triggers dispel fear. Virtually each of the seven triggers will help you overcome your partner's fear. Choosing the most applicable internal triggers and presenting them in the right framework helps to mitigate fear.

The friendship trigger is critical for closure. Trust and confidence develop from friendship, and trust dispels fear. The authority trigger adds confidence and mitigates fear. The conformity trigger reduces fear, since "everybody is doing it." The hope trigger can easily trump fear. Carefully build all of these triggers into your presentation and closure becomes easier for both you and your partner.

At the time of closure, revert to the value profile. Remind your partner what he values and how your proposal meets those values. Since he will be consistent with what he said previously, the consistency trigger alone will play an important role.

ASK FOR AN OPINION

One way to prep for the close during the presentation is to employ the trial close. The trial close is not a close at all; rather it's your thermometer to take the partner's temperature—is it rising toward the close? The trial close asks for an opinion, not a decision. Will people give you an opinion on any element you're discussing? Ask—then try to stop them! We love to give our opinions, and the trial close is a powerful way to assess our progress. A positive opinion tells you you're on the right track—a negative opinion means you have more work to do in that area. A positive answer to a trial close often allows you to wrap up the deal right then.

The best way to facilitate the final agreement is to execute the full process well. Then you can naturally assume that the closure you seek is a foregone conclusion. It should be! Continue as if your partner has made the decision you seek, and outline the execution process, the details. If there is no resistance at this point, you're home free!

The assumptive close is the basis for all closing elements. If you don't assume your partner will comply, he probably will not.

A derivative of the assumptive close is the minor point close. We outlined the fears for closing. We fear big decisions more than little ones. So avoid the "big decision"! Let your partner make a minor decision that lets you both know you're moving forward. Rather than saying, "Will you agree to implement these departmental changes?" say, "Should we implement these changes now, or at the beginning of the quarter?" Give your partner an easy choice, yet one that confirms the decision.

There are thousands of "closes" described in many books and courses. You don't need them. Your job is to prepare for, frame, then deliver your presentation in a manner that makes the close a virtual extension of the process.

Plan that extension carefully. Closure is no time to wing it. Know your goal. Plan how you'll finalize the agreement. Don't be counted among that large percentage who just inform and educate. Be a leader who motivates followers who will agree to and act upon your wishes. And if all else fails at the time of closure, *ask* flat out for what you want. In one way or another, request the specific decision to achieve your persuasion goal.

You're a pro—a leader—and successful leaders put closure on their requests. Closure, agreement, and willing compliance precipitate execution. And execution will produce the results you seek from others.

233

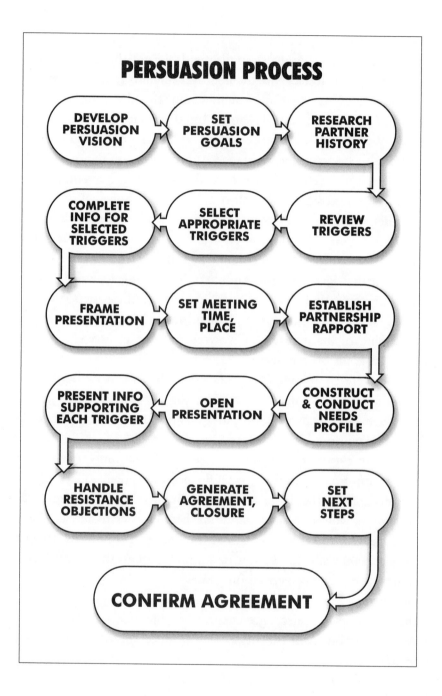

PERSUASION PROCESS

DEVELOP PERSUASION VISION → SET PERSUASION GOALS → RESEARCH PARTNER HISTORY

COMPLETE INFO FOR SELECTED TRIGGERS ← SELECT APPROPRIATE TRIGGERS ← REVIEW TRIGGERS

FRAME PRESENTATION → SET MEETING TIME, PLACE → ESTABLISH PARTNERSHIP RAPPORT

PRESENT INFO SUPPORTING EACH TRIGGER ← OPEN PRESENTATION ← CONSTRUCT & CONDUCT NEEDS PROFILE

HANDLE RESISTANCE OBJECTIONS → GENERATE AGREEMENT, CLOSURE → SET NEXT STEPS

CONFIRM AGREEMENT

REVIEW AND REFERENCE

- Until you trigger "Yes!"—until you get closure on your proposal—you may have nothing to show for your efforts. Fully 63 percent of persuasion presentations end without a request for action.

- Closure is facilitating a firm decision to proceed as proposed. Unless you get closure, you haven't persuaded the decision and action you seek.

- Know your persuasion goal. Write it on the back of your business card. Pull it out before you communicate your presentation, and check it again when you finish.

- You must help your partner reach and acknowledge the desired decision, yet only your partner can make the final decision to say "Yes."

- The number one reason we tarry on that final decision is fear. When activated, our internal triggers dispel fear. Choosing the most applicable internal triggers and presenting them in the right framework help to mitigate fear. Carefully build the emotional triggers into your closing comments.

- At the time of closure go back to the value profile. Remind your partner of what he values and how your proposal meets those values.

- During the presentation, employ the trial close, asking for an opinion, not a decision. A positive opinion tells you you're on the right track—a negative opinion means you have more work to do in that area.

- Try the assumptive approach. Continue as if your partner has made the decision you seek, and outline the execution process. If there is no resistance at this point, you're home free!

- We fear big decisions more than little ones. So avoid the "big decision"! Let your partner make a minor decision that lets you both know you're moving forward.

- There are thousands of "closes" described in the many books and courses on selling. You don't need them. Your job is to prepare for, frame, then deliver your presentation in a manner that makes the close a virtual extension of the process.
- Plan carefully. Know your goal. Plan how you'll finalize the agreement.
- Ask flat out for what you want. Request the specific decision to achieve your persuasion goal.
- For your CPO, current persuasion opportunity, we have an interactive form to help determine the most persuasive elements for your current persuasion goals. Go to www.seventriggers.com where you can select the applicable elements, make notes, and print them out.

Chapter 20

Wrap

We've come a long way together on the road to helping you achieve success through persuasion. We've shared background and breakthrough documentation about the development of persuasion and the new process of more successfully influencing others. We've gone from ancient Greece to the Roman Empire, through the church-controlled dark era, on to Europe, through our early psychology-based faulty guesswork. We've shared today's scientific breakthroughs in brain neurology and their effect on how we help others activate their internal triggers.

We've learned that for some 2,500 years we've been doing it wrong. We've learned that persuasion, the language of leadership, the process of activating internal triggers has been misunderstood and underutilized. We've been privy to expert opinion regarding something we always knew—that persuasion is the core leadership skill and that you can't lead without this skill. And we've learned the good news that now, finally, we have hard science to help us persuade effectively, to get things done with and through others.

We've learned what persuasion really is: a process to reach a shared conclusion. Persuasion is a process, not an event; a process that includes good questioning and listening skills; a process that requires careful framing and delivery of our presentation, with smart handling of resistance, and an absolute requirement to get final commitment.

We've noted that the Chester Carlsons of the world don't get the results the Bill Gateses, Lee Iacoccas, and Jack Welches achieve and now we know why.

It's important to note that the skill of persuasion, the ability to influence others to produce the results you seek, is a critical element in your Emotional Quotient. And that when it comes to getting the desired results, the EQ has been determined to be even more important than the IQ. The concept of EQ in producing management results is a burgeoning concept you'll see more and more about.

Jack Welch weighs in on this issue: "No doubt emotional intelligence is more rare than book smarts, but my experience says it is actually more important in the making of a leader." This is one of the lessons emerging from our new studies of the brain.

As mentioned earlier, Dr. Richard Restak refers to the most important of the suggestions outlined in his book: "Learn as much as possible about how your brain works. This is the most important factor in getting smart and staying smart." Only by understanding how the brain really functions can we know how to influence others' brains and their decision-making process.

Author Tony Jeary adds, "When we understand what makes people receptive to influence, we are in a position to be a motivating force in their lives." Isn't this what you want to become? A motivating force in others' lives?

By recognizing that each and every one of us depends on our own internal self-guidance system to trigger the decisions we need to make every minute of every day, we now understand how to effectively influence others. With intelligent application of the seven triggers, we can help our partner quickly and automatically reach that shared conclusion—the decision to say, "Yes!"

We all crave the power to get things done—to achieve our goals and our dreams. And we know that power comes from getting others to help us achieve results. But as we now know, power is nothing without influence.

You now possess the hard science and the execution skills to persuade—to effectively influence others. The power to influence is in your hands. Wisely apply that power and you will achieve your destiny—wealth, power, and influence.

Persuaders rule—they wield enormous power. They always have. Always will. I wish you every success in achieving a more powerful, influential, and successful life.

Index

Achievers. *See* Innovators
Active listening, 196–198
Adams, John Quincy, 33–34
Adaptation level, defined, 149
Advertising, 55–58, 125–129
Aetna Insurance, 108–109
Agreement. *See* Commitment
Allen, Paul, 21–22
American Management
  Association, 10
American Society for Training and
  Development, 109
Amygdala, 47–49, 55, 61–65, 81
Analysis paralysis, 80–83
Analytical responses, 70–74, 130
Apprentice, The (NBC), 25
Aristotle, 12, 30–31, 68, 107
Arizona State University, 82
Augustine, 33
Authority trigger, 106–120
  activating, 107–108, 115–120
  credibility and, 108–111
  ethos, 68–70
  expertise issues, 111–115
  and risk reduction, 106–107

Authority trigger (*Cont.*):
  as stimulus, 83–86
  summary, 119–120
Automatic responses:
  activating, 83–85
  versus analytical, 70–74
  consistency trigger and, 130

Bargaining. *See* Negotiation
Behaviorism, 35–36, 43–45
Belasco, David, 231
Bell Labs, 19
Blink (Gladwell), 81
Bohnert, Jacqueline, 74
Boyatzis, Richard, 47, 74
Braden, Vic, 82
Brain, human. *See also* Research,
  scientific
  amygdala's role, 61–65
  behaviorist observation, 40–41
  information processing, 3–5,
  6–7
  research, 41–51, 58–61
Brown, Joshua, 62

Russ Granger is founder and president of ProEd Corporation, an international training and consulting company. He has more than 30 years experience in executive management for public and private companies. Russ is a trainer, management consultant, speaker and author specializing in peak performance for sales and management.

His worldwide training and consulting clients form a Who's Who of Fortune 500 clients, plus hundreds of entrepreneurial companies. Russ created research and training partnerships with AT&T's University of Sales Excellence, Prudential, Citigroup, and others.

His speaking engagements have enhanced the performance of executives, managers, and sales professionals throughout the United States, Europe, Australia, Malaysia, New Zealand, Hong Kong, Spain, Singapore, and Canada.

With a degree in psychology, he spent decades researching, writing, and teaching the art and science of persuasion and decision influence.

Russ has two grown children and lives with his wife Janet on Maryland's Eastern Shore.

Contact Us—There's More!

Congratulations! You've completed your personal persuasion journey, and now there are more benefits to explore. It's time to apply the advantage of this breakthrough knowledge to quickly enhance personal and company results.

The critical points of this book—and much more—have been adapted into easily presented one-day seminars and Web-based skills programs that anyone can easily grasp, then apply to specific persuasion opportunities. The programs produce documented results.

These exciting skills programs are designed for individuals and companies who want higher levels of success getting "Yes!" decisions, then desired actions from others.

The 7 Triggers to YES training programs are customized for leaders, managers, and a wide variety of specific sales applications. They are excellent additions to prior training and experience.

To learn more, go to our Web site, www.SevenTriggers.com, where you can find more information about our training, plus you'll find a FREE interactive form to help organize your own Triggers Presentations.

You can contact me at ProEd Corporation's home office:
Email: rhg@proedcorp.com
Voice: 410 819 0303
Fax: 410 770 8745
Mail: P.O. Box[PL1] 1333, Easton, MD 21601
www.seventriggers.com
We can provide you with additional information about:

- Seminar-Based Training Products
- Web-Based Skills Development
- Wholesale Book Orders
- White Papers
- Speaking Engagements
- CDs & DVDs

We have strategic partnership alliances throughout the United States, Australia, India, etc., and we continue to seek additional sales partners for The 7 Triggers to YES training products as well as partners to help develop The 7 Triggers to YES products and training programs for specific industries. Contact me for partner information.

Again, I wish you every success achieving your persuasion goals. Since 1981 we have helped hundreds of companies of every size—from AT&T, Citigroup, Bayer Pharmaceuticals, Sony, Prudential, General Motors and other international giants to mom-and-pop shops—achieve sales, management, and persuasion success. We have helped tens of thousands of sales reps achieve sales peak performance. We can do the same for you. Contact me today!

Cheers,
Russ Granger
President & CEO, ProEd Corp.